IN THE

BELLY

OF

OZ

IN THE
BELLY
OF
OZ

TARZAN KAY

IGUANA

Copyright © 2014 Tarzan Kay
Published by Iguana Books
720 Bathurst Street, Suite 303
Toronto, Ontario, Canada
M5V 2R4

All rights reserved. No part of this publication may be reproduced, stored in a retrieval system or transmitted, in any form or by any means, electronic, mechanical, recording or otherwise (except brief passages for purposes of review) without the prior permission of the author or a licence from The Canadian Copyright Licensing Agency (Access Copyright). For an Access Copyright licence, visit www.accesscopyright.ca or call toll free to 1-800-893-5777.

Publisher: Greg Ioannou
Front cover image and design: Anne-Marie Brouillette
Book layout design: Meghan Behse

Library and Archives Canada Cataloguing in Publication

Kay, Tarzan, author
    In the belly of Oz / Tarzan Kay.

Issued in print and electronic formats.
ISBN 978-1-77180-048-8 (pbk.).--ISBN 978-1-77180-049-5 (epub).--
ISBN 978-1-77180-050-1 (kindle).--ISBN 978-1-77180-051-8 (pdf)

    1. Kay, Tarzan--Travel--Australia. 2. Australia--Description and travel. I. Title.

DU105.2.K39 2014	919.404'72	C2014-901903-3
		C2014-901904-1

This is a first print edition of *In the Belly of Oz*.

This is for Zion.

Prologue

There are some journeys where you hardly know where you're going until you come out the other side. Even then, you won't necessarily know you've arrived until long after the fact. And the further you venture into your future, the deeper you'll have to dive into your past. Once you've really plunged into the muck and squalor of it all, the only way out is to try to make some sort of peace with it and begin to let go. The letting go part is learned; you have to practice. You have to keep learning it every single day.

No matter how bad the place you came from is, its familiarity makes it far less menacing than the uncertainty of the place you are going to. In fact, the more uncomfortable your past, the more likely you are to be carrying it with you — a ready-made explanation when things don't work out the way you planned.

And so it was that upon leaving for Australia I took all of my nitty-gritty, rotten little secrets with me, packed them into a bundle, and zipped them into my heart before tucking into a long flight across the ocean.

Having flung myself from the wicked little nest of my invented self, I blaze ahead blindly, head down and legs pumping; inevitably running smack into everything I was running from.

That's the thing about geography; your emotional baggage is wiped all over the map even before you get to your destination. No matter where you go, your spirit is there, waiting in the wings. However, with the benefit of distance you are free to survey certain things from a more objective view point. It becomes easier to pinpoint where you went off the tracks and locate a new point of entry. As your wounds begin to congeal, you gather together the broken bits and pieces until eventually there's a whole where once was a fragmented thing. You might even give yourself credit for the magnitude of what you are attempting to overcome.

There'll be a string of fresh heartbreaks along the way. Each day you'll turn over some long forgotten rock and find fresh horror lurking beneath. But from that place of wholeness springs a wealth of forgiveness, and that's where the real magic happens. As your spirit strengthens you get down to the business of burying the hatchet — anywhere and everywhere, people, places, things, and everything you ever held a grudge against. You forgive, over and over again, until there is only light and joy. It's like painting a grey sky blue, or digging out the sun from under a pile of rocks. It's like dunking your frozen spirit in a warm bath.

That was Australia in a nutshell; the country that gave back to me everything I'd lost along the way and that filled my pockets with abundance. I arrived a half and came back a whole. Like any journey of self-discovery, I came back with a heart so full of unexpected treasures I could hardly remember what I'd lost in the first place.

PART ONE

HERVEY BAY, QUEENSLAND

The Beginning

(and the end, of course, but mostly the beginning)

The neighbours are drunk again. They're lying on the fire escape in yesterday's clothes, the same neighbours who sell drugs to the youth of Verdun, who traipse up and down our shared staircase at all hours of the night, who broke into my apartment six months ago. I don't even care about the stuff they stole, their dogs who bark at 4:00 a.m., their drunk friends – none of it.

Squinting down at my cell phone in the blazing sun, I've been perched on the fire escape for hours, surveying the back alleys of skid row and waiting for something to happen. After exchanging a series of banal text messages with César, who can't get out of work and won't be stopping by for any final farewells as promised, I climb back into the kitchen and pull down the shades. The bright August sunlight is mocking me. All this time I've been secretly hoping that in some desperate act of chivalry he would finally offer to drive me to the airport. I've been so hung up on the idea that I refused offers from three people, still clinging to the idea of a big romantic send-off at the departures gate.

Retreating to the bedroom, I plummet to the floor, surrounded by neatly folded piles of clothing, carefully stacked packages of chewy candies, the skateboard I built last summer, and a few other non-essential nostalgia items, and commence unpacking and repacking my suitcases for the eighteenth time in as many days. It was my hope that I would be at this very moment returning the room to its former state of disarray, César and I crying out with pleasure while the gifts and candies and clothes were kicked about the room in the heat of passion. Afterward he would profess his love for me, tell me he would wait for me, and perhaps even beg me not to go, our naked bodies desperately clinging to one another, Pale-Skinned Lady and Latino Ken Doll, in a scene worthy of a Harlequin romance novel.

Of course I would leave anyway. I have to go. Not even this invented passion can stop me. It's a trip I've been putting off for ten years — a temporary retreat from my flailing academic career in exchange for a semester of sand, surf, and sister. Besides, I don't actually want to stay; I just want someone to want me to stay, which is not at all the same thing.

~

A doctor once told me we carry our emotions in our livers. I feel it now. This liver of mine is so inflated I can practically feel the weight of it in my hands as it heaves and gags, sifting through various pre-departure anxieties, the old feeling that the entire adventure will be such a lot of work, I might as well stay home where it's cozy and comfortable, where no one expects me to have the time of my life or learn any of life's great lessons.

When the brain detects change, it immediately begins battling against it, sending off a distress signal to the frontal lobe, our creative mother-station, and ordering it to shut down. It's one of the human body's many strange quirks, a proverbial chink in its armour. It's also the reason I bought this plane ticket about five minutes after mounting the whole Australia scheme, certain that if I left my brain even a moment to digest such an extraordinarily imprudent plan of action, it would almost certainly hit the override button.

The thing is I've already given over the last three years to what anyone else would consider "reasonable decision-making." If there's any payoff for such sagacity, I haven't seen it yet. People who sacrifice their lives for their careers are supposed to have cars and money, professionally tinted hair and manicured pets. I have none of those things, which is why I am sitting alone in a roomful of worthless chattels, wondering how in the hell I am going to drag it all to the airport by myself.

I'm impeded by my ego from calling any friends for assistance, since it would mean admitting how grossly I've overestimated the progression of my relations with César, the Latino Ken Doll. How shameful that I'd assumed we had progressed to the drive-each-other-to-the-airport phase and now here he is texting me saying, *Toodaloo Muchacha! See ya when I see ya.* It's humiliating.

I tell myself that real women take the bus. It's a small consolation, and I am careful not to put such declarations under any careful scrutiny. All the same, there's something symbolic about taking yourself to the airport. (Had I known I was embarking on a journey of self-discovery the likes of which would change my life forever, I might even have considered it an honour to escort myself on such an esteemed mission.) No amount of symbolism, however, can keep me from bitching and bellyaching as I drop a spare set of keys in the mailbox and drag three bulging suitcases down four flights of stairs.

From the metro car to the bus station to Trudeau Airport, I continue in the trifling exchange of text messages with César, each as barren as its predecessor. Even at the luggage counter I am still waiting for something to happen, though it's impossible to pinpoint exactly what. I get the feeling of being desperate to eat something delicious, yet no particular snack is especially tempting because I'm not actually hungry. Not for food, anyway. The longing in my heart goes much deeper than any place a minor character like César is likely to reach. The breadth of its bleeding contusions is much greater than anything he is likely to bandage up with a few mundane text messages. But that doesn't stop me from hoping.

~

It seems unfair that air travel gets more and more expensive while we the passengers have to do more and more of the work. Everything is automated now; you have to print your own boarding passes, weigh and tag your own suitcases, even throw them on the conveyor belt. It wouldn't be such a hardship but for the fact that I've been texting round the clock for days and I really just need someone to look me in the eye and talk to me, even if it's only to determine whether or not I'm travelling with any syringes or flammable liquids.

So I stand in the old-fashioned line with all the old ladies and wait my turn, even declining instruction from the battalion of customer service agents attempting to rush things along. I've been suffering fits of anxiety all afternoon. When I couldn't think of an excuse to unpack and repack my suitcases yet again, I left the house four hours early. With time to spare, I consider "accidently" scattering a sheath of loose papers all over the floor and making a big deal about picking them up, just to attract that extra bit of attention I am craving so badly. I content myself with spending ten minutes saran-wrapping my skateboard onto my bag, hoping someone might mistake me for an actual skater and simultaneously dreading that someone else will call my bluff (I can't actually skate).

It's no surprise that my carry-on is five kilos over the limit; between the collected works of Henry James and the caloric equivalent of Willy Wonka's chocolate factory, I'm not even sure how I got it up on the counter. Cheered on by a chorus of groaning from the thirty-odd people lined up behind me, I begin redistributing among my suitcases, not altogether averse to the attention. In a vanishing act worthy of Houdini himself, I manage to force a laptop, a trilogy of teen fiction, and a kilo of Twizzlers into my already overstuffed purse, thus reducing the weight of the offending luggage to a cool nine point nine kilos. The agent graciously does not weigh my conspicuously bulging handbag, if you can still call it that.

~

Even with all the dawdling and attention grabbing, I make it through the gate with two and a half hours left to kill. Against my better judgement, I drift into the airport bookstore and purchase yet another copy of *Mr. Good Enough*, a book that I cannot seem to shake even after having returned it on two separate occasions. At first I found it disturbing and even a little grotesque to think that we women should call off the search for Prince Charming and settle for someone who's kind and has a job, but after a string of X-rated and ill-fated love affairs that went nowhere, I'm starting to think there might be something to it. I settle into the grey expanse of airport benches and, in between more texting with the Latino Ken, wonder if my Harlequin playmate might actually be "Mr. Good Enough," or if he is simply "Mr. Good Enough for Now." The two are easily confused.

Departure is half an hour behind schedule, shortening what is already a criminally brief layover before the long haul to Sydney. By the time I've boarded the plane, sent a few final pea-brained texts and shut off my phone, the last of my energy is sapped. Mercifully, the budget-minded airline is at least clear on where the everyman's values lie: a very welcome TV screen hums in front of me, broadcasting everything from big budget Hollywood glamour to the sort of arty French films that make you sound smart at dinner parties. It's a long trip and I'm tired of sounding smart, I want to be common for a change, so I select one of the former. As soon as I get the chance, I knock back a few glasses of wine and melt into my chair for the next six hours.

The plane touches down about ten minutes before my connecting flight is scheduled to hit the runway. All of the Australia-bound passengers are loaded onto golf carts and zoomed across the airport to the international terminal; the reckless speeding through the blue corridors of the Vancouver airport makes me feel just a little VIP.

The aircraft is remarkably humane. I have two seats to myself, which thrills me. Technically the second is not exactly mine, but as it appears unoccupied I snatch the extra pillow and blanket and sprawl across both seats with exaggerated fatigue. It's late, I'm excited, and my heart is sore in a way that can only be soothed by a few hours in the foetal position. Not even scrunched up knees, recycled air, or knobby airplane seats can keep me from sleep.

~

I couldn't calculate how long I slept even if I tried. By now I must have crossed at least three time zones. For posterity, I assure myself it must have been five or six hours and then drop the subject; if I start making calculations it will be more like forty-five minutes. I scoot out of my seat to do a lap around the cabin, pausing near the emergency exit to do a series of exercises in front on an old man and his disapproving wife. What's a girl to do? You've got to keep the blood flowing.

Somewhere over Guam or Honolulu, I start thinking again of the lover I left behind and I am swept up in a moment of panic, *"Wait! I'm in love, I'm in love, turn the plane around!"* Rather than create mass hysteria in an enclosed space 30,000 feet above ground, I resolve to write him a love letter on a scrunched-up bit of boarding pass, which is the only paper I have handy. The letter comes out as messy and convoluted as the paper on which I am writing, a not-at-all-sexy mish-mash of tangled emotions.

In the end, I decide that I am delusional and prematurely jet-lagged since it's much more convenient than falling in love with someone between whom I am about to put four months and seven thousand miles of distance. I scratch out the scary stuff, crumple up the note and jam it into a damp coffee cup, which gets crammed into the bottom of the makeshift aerial garbage pile that I've already been working on for a few hundred kilometres. If the cabin attendant cares enough about the affairs of my reckless and dishevelled heart to fish a soiled love letter from a sticky coffee cup under a heap of rubbish, I applaud her entrepreneurial spirit. I'm dog-tired, and not in the mood for any ritual burning.

~

I've conveniently forgotten or ignored all the travel tips I so painstakingly sought out before getting on the plane. All except one, that is, and it proves to be more useful than I could have imagined: brush your teeth non-stop. Over the course of the next twenty hours, I become convinced this is the secret of long distance travel. I brush my teeth after every nap, in every airport, after every meal. When I get too groggy or cranky I brush my teeth. If I feel too hungry or too full I brush again. Inevitably, after fifteen hours of stagnant air, over-salted and pre-packaged space food, cramped-up legs and too many Katherine Heigl movies, there are air traffic complications and we have to fly around in a holding pattern for an extra 45 minutes. I'm too excited to care; I'm about to land on the other side of the world and reunite with my long-lost sister, who I've not seen in over two years. Nothing can touch me now.

Minutes before the plane touches down in Sydney, we fly by the Harbour Bridge and the Opera House. I spin around and jab my neighbour just a little bit too hard, "*THE OPERA HOUSE, THE OPERA HOUSE,*" I yell at full, inappropriate-for-air-travel volume. I hardly even care that I've just exposed myself to thirty rows of passengers as a lame imitation of a world traveller. My neighbour throws me a bone, smiling obligingly and looking out the window.

~

By the time I deplane, pass through customs and wait thirty minutes for my luggage at the wrong end of the airport, I'm late checking in for my connecting flight to Brisbane, though it doesn't stop me from recklessly chucking all my belongings onto a cart and bolting across the terminal. It's good to have an excuse to run. I miss the flight. Since it is a popular route, they put me on the next flight; I don't mind having an hour to putter around the airport, brush my teeth and browse the bookstore, absentmindedly wondering if I might return *Mr. Good Enough* a third time, making it a retail hat trick.

Feeling myself begin to lose touch with my former identity, I plod around the airport trying to breathe in the full effect of what I've done. Four months ago I was riding a double-decker bus down the 401, drunk on the height, the speed, and the view from the front seat. I'd been sipping on a large double-double, which at the time would have qualified as dinner. In a moment of clarity the likes of which can only be attributed to the winning combination of open road, empty stomach, and caffeine high, I thought maybe I'll chuck it all in and spend a few months on the beaches of Australia. Despite a thunderous clanging of bells in my head, calling me sick and weak and not capable of such things, I called my sister. Rather than demanding to hear the logistics or chastising me for waking her at four in the morning, she simply said, "When are you coming?"

Shuttling back and forth between terminals I have to pass through security again, which is shockingly lax by North American standards. The security guard asks where I am from. "Canada," I tell him.

"Our favourite," he says, and I laugh.

"You say that to all the pretty girls, don't you?" But I secretly believe him.

On the connecting flight to Brisbane they are playing the news since it must be something like noon. They are announcing the latest in sports. Some burly Australian men are running across a wide field with something that looks similar to football.

What could this mysterious sport be? Lacrosse? I am about to tap my neighbour on the shoulder and ask her to enlighten me on this new and innovative game when I suddenly realise…*rugby*! I cross my legs in quiet mortification and thank the gods of travel for having spared me such an embarrassing cultural blunder.

No sooner do I have a chance to knock back a third cup of coffee, when the pilot asks the attendants to prepare the cabin for landing. Before you know it I am frantically pushing my way through the crowd, weaving around the suitcase trolleys and crying babies, tears already clouding up my eyes because there she is just across the way, watching me navigate this one final obstacle course; my flesh and bone, living, breathing, one-and-only sister — Juliana.

Birds Fly over the Rainbow

My sister has specifically requested that I bring her a sizable quantity of Nibs. After three years away, her homesick heart has built them up to something of a delicacy. Immediately upon hitting the road, we crack open a giant packet of these delectable and now rare treats and proceed to eat ourselves sick. We don't know it yet, but this will be a vital part of our interactions for weeks to come.

I keep reminding Juli to stay on the left side of the road. We coast along the main highway with the windows down, hair flapping in the wind, the early morning sun already beating down, hinting at the coming spring. The highway runs along the coast and is just two lanes wide with an occasional passing lane opening up every few kilometres.

I am no more accustomed to Australian driving conventions than I am to being a passenger on the left side. For hours I am convinced we're facing a head-on collision at any moment. It doesn't help that I'm hyper-stimulated and hopped up from all the candies (which I must learn to call "lollies," if I'm to fit in here). Nobody bothers to signal, honk their horn, or even yell and curse and possibly give the finger like any reasonable person would do back home. Australian drivers are much more casual about suddenly revving the engine and pulling up in front of you at the last possible second as though it's the most natural thing in the world to do. My sister's giddy and spasmodic barefoot driving doesn't help either. By the time we pull up to my sister's house in Hervey Bay —four hours up the coast from Brisbane — I've composed and rewritten my last will and testament about eight times.

∼

It's very common in Australia to rise with the sun and return to bed shortly after its descent. It's been suggested that Australians go to bed earlier and sleep longer than any other nation. In my sister's house, bedtime is as early as 8:30 p.m., which suits my jet lag just fine. For an entire week I wake up around 3:00 a.m. and roll around in bed for hours listening to the song of the birds and savouring the smell of cold, salty air and the freshly laundered sheets that hang on the line in the yard. Without an alarm clock in the guest bedroom, I learn to tell time by the birdsong outside my window — at 3:30 a.m. a few meagre tweet tweets, around 4:00 a.m. an atonal melody so eerily human that for days I worry some vagrant is whistling just outside my window, and finally at 4:30 a.m. a choir of noisy lorikeets chirping in the grapefruit tree in front of the house. By the time the bird symphony dies out, it's 6:00 a.m., I'm already onto my second cup of coffee and my sister is peeling herself out of bed to greet the day with a song of her own.

We eat Nibs for breakfast until our stock is exhausted. My sister laughs all the time, even when she is crying and suffering the harshest of disappointments. She has not had an easy marriage. With her husband off at sea, trawling for prawns in far north Queensland, she is alone in an empty house many thousands of miles from everyone she knows for as many as seven months a year. Juli and her husband are free to communicate by satellite phone, but at $3/minute, their conversations do not last long. When the trawler is nearer to the coast they can video chat online, which sounds good in theory but is maddening as all hell in reality. With the service coming in and out, their conversation inevitably goes something like this: *"Hey ba…is that…in range now…can you star…togeth…whe…I got the same…this is so frus...ok, that's beh…can you hear me no…"*

With the two of us shacked up together, this year's tiger prawn season is infinitely more bearable. We laugh and laugh until we're clutching our stomachs and gasping for air. We're like teenagers whose parents are out of town and have decided to throw an all-girl sleepover. We bought ourselves a case of wine and an unlimited supply of lollies. Every mundane activity is in some way hilarious because we do it together. I have the feeling we're breaking the rules; that we're getting away with something bad.

~

My sister and I grew up in a house of many rules; rules about what to wear, rules about which music to listen to, rules about which movies to watch, rules about which books to read. The bulk of these regulations were put in place by our father in a fit of hysteria, the source of which was usually something entirely unrelated. Many of them go back so far that for the most part I was too young or too unaware to connect the dots between cause and effect.

I remember very clearly the morning he suddenly declared that Juli and I were to start wearing dresses every single day; it was unchristian for us girls to be running around in pants all the time. The Closed Plymouth Brethren, with whom our family was in fellowship, were opposed to such worldliness. It was equally frowned upon for women to cut their hair and wear jewelry or make-up. Showing skin was considered especially sinful, though it's unclear where pants came into the picture. Yet we never threw stones where our patriarch was concerned; no one in our family pointed out that it was the nineties or that girls weren't wearing dresses anymore, to church or otherwise.

My parents weren't the sorts of people reading Betty Friedan in the sixties. My father had already begun his missionary work by then while my mother would be shipping off to Bible College before the decade was out. The great mysteries of womanhood were mostly limited to how white she could get her whites or how she made the Corning glassware sparkle like diamonds. For all their worldly expertise, the *Feminine Mystique* might as well have been a Tide campaign.

In retaliation for what she recognised as a directive that defied all logic, our mother demanded a handsome sum for the purchase of new fabrics. She made the most of it by sewing us a closetful of calf-length summer dresses. A born negotiator, she also managed to whittle the dress rule down to every other day. My father liked to say that the only person who can buy from a Gentile, sell to a Jew, and still make a profit is a Mennonite, which my mother was. She negotiated her husband expertly. Eventually she would negotiate us the hell out of there.

Like a good Mennonite wife, she sewed our entire wardrobe from scratch. Many a Friday evening, the eight of us would load into our Dodge Ram van and drive across the border to Joanne Fabrics, where we would spend hours selecting patterns, fabrics, zippers, and buttons. On the way home, we would stop at a roadside dive called Jet Port, where we drank pitchers of Squirt and consumed mountains of chicken wings.

The van was called the *Grey Goose*, for the image our mother had painted on the tire cover in a demonstration of artistic prowess that went almost entirely unexploited for the whole of her married life. The *Grey Goose* could fit my parents, four brothers, my sister and I quite comfortably, probably even two or three more had my mother not insisted on having her tubes tied after I was born. My father, who was opposed to birth control for religious reasons, did not object and, in fact, seemed to breathe a sigh of relief.

For all the concern he expressed for our worldly indulgences, he took very little notice of our daily routine, therefore it was not long before the dress requirement faded into oblivion. Yet he remained an active participant in the moral upholding of the household. By then I was old enough to be privy to some of the internal goings-on of our house and so when my father came up with the idea to screen every cassette tape in the house, I understood the house-politics motivating his actions.

In any case, he made no effort to conceal the source of his rage. How he had come across my mother's copy of Jean Auel's *Clan of the Cave Bear* was anyone's guess. She'd been very careful about keeping it hidden, reading it almost exclusively in the bathroom with the door locked. Even more miraculous is that he opened it to the single page that could possibly have been considered morally questionable – a sex scene.

From upstairs I could hear him raging wildly in the kitchen, *"Gimme all your tapes,"* he cried to my sister and I. *"Gimme all your tapes,"* he repeated. Ever the dutiful youngest daughter, I laid my precious collection of cassettes out on my desk and left the room while he bounded up the stairs and proceeded to confiscate the lot of them. Meanwhile, my sister was busy burying her *Rancid* and *Green Day* cassettes in a cupboard full of jeans and turtlenecks while I stood watching, paralyzed by the fear of discovery.

Our mother allowed him to rage but did not reciprocate. She packed us a suitcase and drove us to her mother's apartment, where we spent the night. We returned the next morning with my mother offering apologies for her defiance. She knew she'd been within her rights to leave, but she valued the harmony of the household more highly than her own vindication. Though none of us women received anything like an apology from the mouth of our patriarch, we found our cassette tapes had been returned overnight.

It wasn't the only time our father convinced himself of the necessity of such censorship. There was never a movie watched in our house without one ear open to the sound of creaking stairs. Our father was prone to tiptoe downstairs to the family room and sit in for a few minutes on whatever it was we were watching. Such surveillance would usually end in a long sermon delivered with elaborate gestures and wild eyes, confiscation of the film and perhaps even further punishment given the severity of the infraction. Major incidents resulted in the confiscation of films such as *Indiana Jones and the Temple of Doom, Ghostbusters, Labyrinth,* and, inexplicably, *The Next Karate Kid.*

For this reason, we owned a number of pre-approved films, which I always preferred since it was only then that we could relax and enjoy the show. Some had biblical themes: *The Ten Commandments, The King and I,* and *Ben-Hur.* We were also permitted such classics as *Spartacus* and *Lawrence of Arabia.*

For some reason my father enjoyed *The Simpsons* and even after having watched it on several occasions never managed to find anything objectionable. Sometimes he would even retell the jokes and compare himself to Homer Simpson, which of course we all found sort of ironic.

~

It's only natural that when a wild animal is caged it will fight like hell to escape, which is what we were and is also what we did. One by one, my siblings flew the coup. My brothers left in quick succession before reaching the age of majority. My sister was the youngest to leave, dropping out of school and fleeing across the country when she was barely fifteen. I was thirteen when she left, which makes fourteen years since we have spent any significant time together.

Now that we *are* together, we don't take it for granted that we can play loud music in the living room and speak freely about anything we like without fear of reprimand. That's what makes it so thrilling to drink wine in the afternoon, bitch and swear and traipse around in our bikinis. Deep down we're still just a couple of Mennonite girls trying to pull the wool over our old Dad's eyes.

~

Eventually I give up; I give in to the rhythm of the rolling tides and rise at 6:00 a.m. with the rest of the world. Australian spring is hardly in evidence at this hour and the house isn't heated. We wrap ourselves in blankets, sweaters and scarves to ward off the cold, peeling them away one at a time as the sunlight meanders into the living room window and the damp air blows out through back door.

Breakfast in our house is a historic event. In fact, we eat breakfast twice daily. Given our small size and number of hours we spend lounging in the backyard, one might think we would skip lunch or dinner, an incorrect assumption. Skipping a meal would be like bailing on an all-expenses-paid trip to Disneyland; each is a momentous occasion.

We start with our homemade cereal blend: mixed seeds and grains with cocoa nibs and goji berries drowned in a pool of rice milk and maple syrup. Later on we cook up a hearty portion of lentils, drenched with coconut oil and topped with eggs, fried onions, garlic, and whatever green vegetables we have handy. It is a hideous brown and green mash that no one not directly born into our family would conceivably agree to eat. But we Knapp women are so busy extolling the extraordinary palatability of our lentil mash we have hardly enough air left to swallow our food, so utterly delectable and seasoned with the company of sisters. So much pleasure, so much joy, I am genuinely gasping for breath.

Over breakfast we plan lunch and dinner and in the afternoons we drive around collecting provisions for our culinary pursuits, snacking all the way. In the evenings we walk my sister's unruly dogs, though it is plainly clear to any passer-by that it is in fact the dogs who are walking us — something the locals are repeatedly compelled to point out to us. We are something of a spectacle; two women the combined weight of a storm cloud, being dragged along the esplanade, our upper bodies inclined backward at least thirty-five degrees, wielding all of our weight against the strength of these wild beasts, Zeddy and Jade.

It was only a matter of time before I figured out that, in Australia, Australian wine is dirt-cheap. At the discount liquor store (of which there are many), you can buy a perfectly drinkable bottle of *Wolf Blass* for $5. I'm not exactly Bill Gates; I came here with $750, I've got no job and no prospects. With that in mind, I only buy two bottles and wait until I've sent at least three official sounding letters each day before kicking up my feet with a glass of cold merlot, which is how they drink it over here.

There are days when Happy Hour starts as early as 10:30 a.m. After we've polished off the *Wolf Blass* we switch to blend of Cab-Merlot called *Bowler's Run*, which you can get for just $3 a bottle, or $2.50 if you buy it by the case, so of course we do. With the early starts, I've already eaten second breakfast and painted the town curriculum vitae grey by 10:00 a.m. Juli is tanning in her bikini in the backyard, ready to pop out for some more lollies.

I like to wait until late afternoon when the sun comes flooding through the living room window and I can twist open a fresh bottle while rehashing the day's "work" with my sister. But every so often I figure what the heck, it's almost noon and I'm all the way on the other side of the Pacific Ocean, who's gonna know?

The Emerald City

The local economy is by no means flourishing. The shopkeepers are mostly singing the same tune; unemployment in Hervey Bay is the worst in the country, business is slow. Empty storefronts decorate the esplanade, stretching out across the bay all the way down to the Boat Club. Having burned through my $750, mostly on lollies, *Bowler's Run* and the occasional case of *XXXX Gold*, destitution is unnervingly close at hand.

In the spirit of economy, I pick up a manual from the library on how to stretch a dollar, thinking I'll take a pre-emptive strike at my impending doom. It's full of sound advice, like "spend more time at the park" and "pack your own lunches." Since my sister and I are both unemployed we mostly just lay on the beach, returning to the house twice a day at mealtimes. But then there's that dreadful bit about making your own lattes and, worst of all, saving your wine for special occasions. In protest I pour myself a liberal glass of red, the $5 stuff, which is still cheaper than orange juice really, and determine things will be different for us. Surely we will find jobs and be rolling in money before the week is out.

We soldier on unhindered by all the talk and things begin to work out. Juli is invited for interviews all over town and eventually scores a job waiting tables down at the Boat Club. Maybe it's not her dream job, but in a town where unemployment is nearing twenty-five percent, it's more than what a lot of people can boast. Just as the money is really running out, a few odd jobs begin to trickle in for me too: French teacher, piano teacher, supermarket sample girl, legal assistant, etc. One particularly auspicious morning, I score two jobs simultaneously and still manage to spend most of the day at the beach. It seems our own personal economy is flourishing.

In the late afternoon, our living room is flooded with light for two exquisite hours. It is here that we have our best conversations, bathing in the warmth of the sun and laughing until we're blue in the face. Juli attempts to explain the finite differences between AFL (Australian Football League), rugby league, and plain old rugby. They all look like football to me; it's impossible to tell the difference given the ball is the same in all three games. No one wears anything remotely resembling the padded up, NFL-style protective gear I am accustomed to seeing. More importantly, it's hard to focus on anything that's going on when the players are so very burly and handsome and parading around in such very short shorts. To boot, Juli's own understanding of the game is clumsy at best and mostly based on speculation, having presumably been similarly distracted by said athletes in skimpy outfits.

By the end of week two, we have formally instituted Arts & Crafts Hour. Some evenings Juli practices piano while I yell instructions from the couch. Other days she sketches tree frogs in the living room while I write, play a little music, or draft the odd love letter for later use mopping up an overturned glass of wine or folding into an emotionally charged bookmark.

In the evenings when I am tired I begin to miss my lover. Communication with César becomes more and more infrequent until it dwindles to almost nothing at all. On days when he condescends to an instant message, it is usually no more than one or two phrases. Ever the cheerleader for love, I respond with six paragraphs full of undisguised hope and longing. It takes little more than the idea of love to bring all of my honesty and vulnerability bubbling to the surface, which of course makes me infinitely less attractive to Latino Ken, who is not about to go without simply because Barbie decided to take a little holiday.

It takes almost three weeks to figure out that Ken had thrown in the towel even before the plane took off. While I was composing messages of love from the departure gate, in all likelihood Ken was making a date for the following Saturday. To be fair, I've been pretending not to see this coming. Between his failure to escort me to the airport and neglecting to give even a proper farewell, the writing was on the wall. It doesn't make it hurt any less. Ever the dutiful sister, Juli doesn't say anything when I blast sad music for three days straight and quietly looks the other way when I pour a third or fourth glass of wine.

Sometimes losing the idea of love is as bad as losing the love itself. Days when the stinging in my heart gets the better of me, I throw on my swimsuit and go running barefoot down the road, cross the beach and launch myself into the ocean. I march home soaking wet, tripping on my sarong, feet scorching on the hot pavement, feeling just a little bit lighter.

~

We give up wearing pants when the weather reaches twenty-eight degrees. We learn to gauge the temperature by the consistency of the coconut oil in our kitchen. When the oil gets soft and liquid-y, we declare it a no-pants day and hang around the house in our knickers all afternoon. The temperature is set to reach thirty degrees on Friday so we plot an afternoon expedition to one of the bay's better beaches, our first of the season.

We organise the particulars of this excursion with enough detail to necessitate a dress rehearsal Thursday afternoon. Straight out of the gate, my sister reprimands me for having made some rookie mistakes: too many snacks and not enough beer, too much sunscreen and not enough exposed skin to ensure an even tan. This will be corrected on Friday when I really step up my game, correcting the beer-to-snack ratio and selecting a skimpier swimsuit. Our beach trip is a success, of course, as we have had plenty of practice. The wind is high, the tide is in, and by now we have discovered boogie boards. Life will never be the same again.

Every single day is charged with what can only be described as an abundance of abundance. It is perpetually nipping at our heels. One afternoon we're driving down the highway when we realise the road ahead is casually snaking through the arch of a rainbow. It's like driving into the gates of heaven. The clock reads 11:11 and I can't think of a thing to wish for. People don't even wear shoes here. The under thirty population of Hervey Bay is padding around barefoot. Lemonade actually grows on trees in the form of sweet lemons.

We become overwhelmed. Can a person have too much abundance? My back aches from all the lounging on the beach. Life is so good I begin to feel anxious. A holiday such as this is a lot like new love — equal parts ecstasy and terror. You get so high it seems the only place to go is down. On the beach, we declare we absolutely *must* go home and relax. Tomorrow we'll take a day off going to the beach. What I mean is, we'll take a day off taking a day off.

Love You Forever, Love You for Always

My father had a stroke seven days before I left for Australia. That very afternoon we'd been eating lemon meringue pie in his backyard, in the peeling green Adirondack chairs of our youth. Three generations sat carefully navigating this infamous package dessert — a bachelor's variation of the pie my mother used to make him and the subject of some derision amongst my siblings — as we watched my father's grandchildren playing in the yard, trolling for bugs in the neighbours' grass.

That evening he slept in his bed and not in his chair as he usually does; the frayed and fading blue lounge chair that's been in the family since I was in knee pants. Back then it didn't belong to him quite so much as it does now. Only in the last ten years has it become as much an extension of himself as any of his limbs: the signature piece in the basement apartment where he lives, to his right a record player and to his left a stack of books a mile high, his mother's bible at its zenith.

At three o'clock in the morning my father fell out of bed, crawled to the phone and called the fourth of his six sons. No answer. Next he tried his neighbour, Ron. Any other day Ron's wife might have slept through rubblizing concrete in the next room, but tonight, miraculously, she woke to the sound of the ringing handset. By this time, my Dad was fading fast. *I'm having a stroke*, he mumbled, three times, before losing consciousness.

She might not have understood his warbling tones but his name was on the caller ID and it was the middle of the night. Even if my father does tend toward melodrama from time to time, he does not wake friends from slumber without just cause. For all his emotionalism and romanticism, he is a practical man.

My mother drove me to the hospital but for reasons I hardly understood at the time chose not to come in. My eldest brothers had arrived earlier and were taking turns going in and out of the ER. My father was alone when I went in to see him, and he instantly melted into tears, looking up at me with the eyes of a frightened child. The left side of his watery, old man face was drooping to the side as he murmured, *I lost the power of speech*, and then crumbled into more silent weeping.

The nurse warned us that victims of strokes are often emotional. In his old age, my Dad is already a sentimental fellow. At eighty-four, his ears no longer hear as well and his fingers no longer dance along the piano keys the way they did when I was a child. Even his voice has developed a characteristic croakiness in the last few years, further amplified by his stroke. His heart though, feels things more acutely than ever.

~

In the last half decade or so, every phone conversation I've had with my father has invariably begun with what he calls the "organ recital," the one where he goes through each of his bones and vital organs, tells me where he is aching and how he's been treating it. Next we might talk about the nursing homes where he's done his "visitations" and the friends with whom he has engaged in bible study. Even in his ripe old age, his social calendar is much livelier than my own. A bachelor for many years now, he has enjoyed over a decade of solitude and since his retirement must have engaged in many an hour of quiet reflection, the result of which is a softer, more emotive version of the man I grew up with. The smallest acts of kindness and the most minute professions of love will move him to tears, particularly if they are offered by any of his nine children.

Anyone who's paying attention would see that my father is plagued with regret. Unaccustomed as he is to discussing his feelings, his stroke only served to emphasize the obvious fact that all this pent-up emotion has packed his heart so tightly, something had to burst if it was to continue beating. My father dedicated the entirety of his life's work to the spiritual salvation of others, starting with his own children. Before the death of his first wife and subsequent career change, he worked as a travelling missionary for thirty years. A leader among his spiritual brethren, he is highly revered not only by his own people but also in the broader religious community. His progeny, on the other hand, are exactly the rebellious band of miscreants you would expect to grow out of a strict religious upbringing.

The history of our family reads like an unfortunate grocery list of every unchristian act you can think of; drug addiction, jail time, an array of illegal business endeavours, babies born out of wedlock, teenage runaways, divorce, bootlegging, a seemingly endless inventory of obscene performances that would bring shame to any family, Closed Plymouth Brethren or otherwise.

The extreme juxtaposition of the lives we led versus the lives he would have chosen for us created an enormous chasm between my father and his children. More and more subjects became taboo until honest and open conversation was essentially impossible. So it was that most of us left home barely teenagers, unable to cope with the fury and disappointment of our father incurred on the occasion of our respective failures.

For my father's part, he would often escape south of the border where he could break bread with his Brothers in Christ in a place that was for the rest of us an alternate universe where everyone understood and obeyed all the rules. He would pass months at a time in New Jersey with the Brethren, ostensibly for work. The Brethren regularly hired him to paint their houses over the holidays, taking him away from his children over Christmas, which was particularly problematic at our house. To this day my father has strong feelings about the true meaning of *"Xmas,"* as he likes to call it, with a particular emphasis on the *X*.

My siblings and I felt particularly hard done by at Christmas, which we were forbidden to celebrate given its modern disassociation with Christ. There were no bells or coloured lights or Christmas trees in the Knapp house, though my mother did her best to wrap a few meagre trinkets and deliver them inconspicuously on Christmas Eve. On such occasions, our father would retreat to the basement in protest; enraged he could not induce even his own wife to forgo these heathen traditions.

It was in this way we drifted away, one from the other, until the most my father could expect from his children were one or two phone calls a year, and sometimes none at all. My own relationship with him is unique, however. The youngest of his multitudinous brood, I was easily the most eager to please and the fastest to turn my gaze in the face of conflict. Perhaps more importantly, I followed the rules, at least on the surface of things.

Long before I was old enough to intentionally misbehave or even question the system of beliefs he'd laid in place for his family's salvation, the two of us were busy laying the foundation of our own relationship. It was laid, brick by brick, on our Sunday trips to the candy store, two junk-food lovers strolling hand in hand to the secular promised land of Mars Bars and

Cheese Twisties. In later years we had music in common and as such had never to fear dead air on the other end of the line, which is more than I can say for my siblings. As an adult, there would always be an edition of Beethoven's *Sonate Pathétique* or a volume of Debussy missing from my collection, something I needed for school. At worst, we could always be two pianists sharing a love of Chopin.

~

So it was me that sat with him for hours in the ER that day. Our family's relationship with the Plymouth Brethren is one of implied mutual disapproval, one where we each have the courtesy to ignore the other and thus avoid a lot of unnecessary friction. My siblings and I do not share (nor have we ever shared) cell numbers, home numbers, addresses, or any other information of such a nature with the Brethren. We prefer to quietly survey one another from the safe distance of our moral high-horses, the international border our unsung referee. It is a comfortable sort of cease-fire that has functioned more or less adequately for two decades. Until now, that is. Ergo, I spent the afternoon fielding calls on the ER's landline until the nurses understandably began to lose patience and cut me off. Cousins I'd never heard of called all the way from California. In addition to his battalion of Brothers in Christ, every name on my father's busy calendar called hourly, demanding updates.

Under the glaring fluorescent lights of the hospital emergency unit, my father seemed to age ten years in as many hours. He's always been an old man, even when I was a child. Yearly, we would go for family photos and the photographer would squint into his camera saying things like, "turn your head an inch to the left, sweetheart, toward your ol' granddad." I never minded. As a child, the difference between thirty-five and fifty-five is nothing. Adults are adults and kids are kids. But as my twenties rolled along, my Dad very suddenly morphed into a genuine "elderly man." He embraced his old age and for the first time in his life truly began to act the part.

As a recently divorced man of seventy-something, he bought himself a motorised scooter and began motoring around town with geriatric gusto even though his legs were still more than capable. He relished being diagnosed with diabetes since it finally gave him a credible excuse to avoid eating brown rice. True to form though, he could never refuse an after-dinner dose of something sweet. When he repeated the same stories over and over, he would jump at the opportunity to remind me that old age and senility are a proverbial horse and carriage. After more than a half-century of hard work and grave responsibility, my father had finally given himself permission to age. And so aged he has, not only with acceptance but also with plain, unadulterated enthusiasm.

Melodramatic as he is, my father has been known to cry wolf. The word "stroke" was taken lightly. Bent as he was on convincing us of his advanced age, we were working on the assumption he'd merely suffered a TIA (*transient ischemic attack*, commonly known as a *mini-stroke*) and not in fact a full-blown now's-the-time-to-say-your-last-words stroke. Even after tests confirmed that what our father had suffered was indeed the real McCoy, for hours we all clung to the idea that he would return home in a few days and resume business as usual. One of the more candid nurses eventually set us straight when she casually raised the issue of where our father would live once he had finished a course of rehabilitation and suggested some nursing homes that might be admitting new residents. Rehabilitation? Nursing home? These were new ideas for all of us, my father included.

It's not always easy to pinpoint the exact moment when you cease being the cared for and become the carer of an aging parent. That day in the hospital I held my father's hand and offered what comfort I could while he struggled, through many tears shed from the deepest core of his anguished heart, to relay the events of the day, to make some sense from what was happening, to find a peaceful resolution to his past, present and future all in the span of this one historic day. Many hours were passed in this way; my long, girlish fingers lay on his speckled and veiny hand until he eventually took himself far enough past the point of exhaustion that sleep came effortlessly. In this exchange was a silent pact between parent and child:

Now that I am old and my body is weak, I will let go and fall into the arms of sleep with the tender certainty that from this point on, you will be my guardian.

At every meal in every wing of the hospital – the emergency room, the stroke unit, the rehabilitation centre – he would say something to the effect of its being nothing like my mother's cooking. After twenty-five years of marriage and twelve of divorce, my father has never spoken a nasty word about his wife, which is how he still thinks of her even after all these years. He praises her skills as a homemaker and similarly grabs at any opportunity to remind us what a wonderful mother she was, and still is. At the hospital he calls her by her middle name, Kay, which is the closest thing to a term of endearment in my father's lexicon but one that fell out of use after the dissolution of their marriage.

My mother visits him also, once the shock has been absorbed. He introduces her to the nurses as his wife. Given that she is twenty-four years his junior and looks ten years younger still, the nurses are justifiably perplexed. Where my father's skin is wrinkled and covered in liver spots, my mother's is clear and luminescent, the very picture of youth and vitality. Where my father likes to wear tattered sweater vests with socks and sandals poking out under faded khaki pants, my mother dresses in brightly coloured knee high boots and loudly printed scarves. A vision in leather pants, she is unmistakably in her salad days while my father is as unequivocally in the winter of his life.

A more distinct pair of formerly-marrieds, you cannot imagine. You can almost hear the nurses wondering to themselves if my father is perhaps a wealthy sugar daddy, or lost in the throes of dementia. Graciously, my mother smiles and nods along — reluctant to publically remind my father in his deteriorated condition that she is not in fact his wife anymore, nor would the suggestion be especially flattering to her given his current condition — and later at the nurses' station, we apprise them of the situation in hopes of avoiding any legal or medical confusion.

As the nurse expressed to us with unvarnished clarity, our father will not be returning home anytime in the foreseeable future, if he is indeed to return at all, which is unlikely. My sister-in-law and I make a day trip to Niagara-on-the-Lake to rescue his perishables and pack an overnight bag so that he will at least have the comfort of the Good Book for his soul, slippers for his feet, and the knowledge that his cat, Heidi, is fed and watered. In his fridge we uncover all sorts of delightfully undiabetic food. Lo! A half-drunk bottle of beer sits in the fridge!

My father is a notorious teetotaller who delights in reminding us that he was only once in his life reduced to a state of inebriation. A client had mixed him a strong one that he unknowingly gulped down before proceeding to fall asleep under a tree, overcome with drink — my father the alky. So it is with unrestrained glee that we observe this alien item in his refrigerator, savouring firstly that it is in fact real, Canadian lager and not the .05 "Christian Beer" he permitted himself in his day, and secondly that he is still the lovably irredeemable amateur barfly, screwing the lid back on a half-consumed bottle, as though it might do better to age another day or two. It seems that even in their eighties, your parents can still surprise you.

Thumbing through a stack of books on his bedside table, I select one at random and find under the jacket a handwritten note. "Zoloft — *depression*," it says in looping, lead pencil letters at the upper left hand corner of a folded 8" x 12" sheet of white paper. It is not my father's handwriting. The thought of my father being not only depressed, but also alone in the basement apartment where he sits up some nights until 2:00 a.m., shakes my heart so grievously I may need some *Zoloft* myself. Left to imagine the circumstances of this note, my powers of ingenuity fail me. To whom would my father open his heart in such a way? Who is this mysterious stranger, the author of this grave diagnosis?

Far as I can stretch my imagination, it does not extend to my father using the actual word "depression," and certainly not in reference to himself. But then given my his substantial emotional development over the years, I can almost hear the word rolling off his tongue in the awkward way it does when you are saying a word aloud for the first time, as in the first time you say a word like "sex" or "puberty" — a word that, incidentally, my father used in conversation with me only once and pronounced "poo-berty" — and much as you would will it otherwise, it has a distinct throaty quality, the consonants particularly cumbersome. As it happens, the idea that he is indeed depressed is all too easy to justify — disturbingly so.

Faced with the reality of our father's failing health, the family starts discussing where he might live post-rehabilitation. Across the border, the Brethren are having a similar conversation. For years now they have been plotting to snap him up for themselves, rescue him from our worldly family. Bent as they are on housing and nurturing my father in his golden years, he's been reluctant to accept their generous offer, not only given the staunch opposition from his children but also because he has spent decades building a life in Canada, and that life is not such a bad one. And yet an offer like that would be hard to refuse for a man of his age so he has been seesawing back and forth about it for a good while.

Among the Brethren, my father is offered the ultimate vindication and the reverence that he must in some subconscious way feel he deserves: the Father, the Son and the Holy Mr. Knapp. From their perspective, his every familial manoeuvre has been perfectly justifiable and right in the eyes of the Lord. Theirs is a community where nearly every article of faith is shared, speckle-for-speckle, down to the finest detail. Contentious points of ecclesiastical doctrine have been debated to the nth degree and those with opposing ideas have either willingly defected or been publicly ostracised. Not surprisingly, their community is very small and diminishing further with each passing year. The righteous couple contending to house my father has already blacklisted not only their own parents on both sides but also their children along with their spouses and grandchildren. So whittled down is this group of believers, they have been reduced to poaching long absented members all the way from Canada.

I wonder if my father isn't past the point of blind absolution. Maybe in your old age it becomes preferable to face up to your failures and rejoice in small victories. In any case, the moment my father is moved into a semi-private room with his own telephone line, the Brethren start lobbying hard and this time the gloves are off. They ring him four times a day, lulling him with offers of a private residence, a full meal package, access to transportation any time of day and, most tantalising of all, the promise of daily bible study in the comfort of like minds and the opportunity to break bread with his peers every evening for the remainder of his days. Not a bad deal if you ask me, particularly for a man who has given everything and I do mean everything — his marriage, his career, his children and grandchildren — to the worship of God and the sanctity of divine grace. There is only one elephantine catch; he must leave his family behind. Though this little snag is not explicitly stated, it is undeniably inferred from the subtext of our family history. My wayward siblings and I have been tacitly unwelcome in their homes for years.

Sometime in the nineties, my mother's controversial beliefs became common knowledge among the Brethren. In a subtle sort of excommunication, they generously allowed that she would still be welcome in their homes if only at mealtimes she would submit to being seated at a separate table and served only bread and water. After the truth came out, they took the occasion to step back and observe while, one by one, the entirety of the Knapp family hurled themselves from the spiritual grain train only to plant their stolen seeds on the wrong side of the biblical tracks. Since that day, only one of my unruly siblings has dared to visit these fine people.

No longer able to bear their callous attitude toward the unity of our family, somewhere I find the courage to ring one of the offending Brothers on the telephone. Calmly, I attempt to explain how much my father is loved and cared for in Canada. The New Zealand faction of our family has crossed fourteen thousand miles to keep him company in his golden years. In

America, he would have no family, no friends, and, more practically speaking, no health care. But this Brother's ears are closed. Rather than listening half-heartedly or even condescending to patronise me with a bit of feigned deliberation, he proceeds to quote me a long sermon, finally insisting, *the Lord will guide him in his decision.*

I too subscribe to a similarly benign approach to conflict resolution, so I sympathised with the man's thickheaded assessment of the situation. But it was my father's future at stake. I was not about to take a backseat to this philosophical bullying. Not this time. My father is easily influenced under the best of circumstances, but his trusting nature made him a hundred times more malleable in his deteriorated state. It was plain to see that the pressure they were putting on him had critically overwhelmed his depleted spirit. So acutely conscious was he of the magnitude of their offer, he would almost accept it rather than offend them with a refusal. Over and over he expressed a desire to honour their offer, for his spiritual family and his earthly family to sit down together and "sort out" the situation.

These conversations formed the basis of my discussion with this stubborn Brother, though *discussion* is hardly the right word since talking with that man was like pounding cement with my bare fists — all pain and no reaction. This bland exchange quickly devolved into verbal sparring. In desperation, I called attention to the hard fact that they had appropriated our patriarch over every holiday and every special occasion since we were children and perhaps it was our turn to spend a little time with the man who had given life to us. With calculated coldness, he retorted, *I understand you yourself are leaving for Australia for several months.* When I finally hung up the phone, my entire body was pulsating with rage.

I suppose in the end my father was indeed directed by some divine guidance. Six months later, he is happily settled in one of the very senior's residences where he once made weekly visits. Not only is it tremendously comforting to see my father settled in such close proximity to his friends and family, I can't help but indulge in just a bit of smug satisfaction knowing that from a decades-long battle with what a more diplomatic person might resist calling a bitter foe, our family has emerged victorious.

A week after my father's brush with the impending conclusion at which we all must arrive eventually, I boarded a very big plane and flew halfway around the world. What can I say in my defence; that it felt right at the time? That my sister needed me as much as he did? I'd like to say my father would've wanted it this way but part of me doubts that. No more can I compile a list of pros and cons for my departure than I can honestly say what propelled me this far away from my ailing father, except that the deed was done with equal parts courage and cowardice.

For elderly people, or any people for that matter, the first stroke is often the warm-up act the next, more spectacular stroke. The idea that my father could "go at any time" has been a constant in our lives for years already. In the last decade my relationship with this man has been one of mutual affection and cheerful benevolence. There are no enormous secrets or heartfelt apologies lurking under the surface. The things that needed to be shared have been shared. In the week before I left, more tears were shed and more genuine professions of love were offered than have been in years. Though my father plainly craves understanding and forgiveness from his children, I have given these things to him in as much as I am capable. I hold no grudges.

We Knapps are a stubborn bunch, prone to soak in the muck of our quiet grievances. Even if he might've wanted it otherwise, in his heart of hearts I doubt that he faults me for going ahead with the Australia scheme. He keeps my letters in his shirt pocket and I can just picture him taking them out and reading them to anyone who will listen. If he can't read them himself, he will have his guests read them aloud to him. Rather than taking pity on himself at having been callously abandoned by his youngest child, he will take pride in his gypsy daughter, gallivanting halfway around the world. He'll wave the letter around like a flag. *My daughter loves me!* How can I explain how proud I am of my father? Not just for being so proud of us but for allowing himself to take pride in anything, let alone his mercilessly disobedient offspring.

It takes so very little to please him, to bring joy to his once troubled heart. If my sister calls, he will tell me about it every time we speak for the ensuing month. This ceaseless repetition could easily be chalked up to old age and senility but I come from the same flesh and blood as this man so I know better. His unfailing redundancy disturbs me because it so clearly demonstrates how deprived he has been of the love of his children and how much he must crave it. Had he known that candy bars and music scores were the seeds of a healthy paternal plant, he probably would have sowed them sooner. For all I know it takes having nine children to finally get the hang of it.

However imperfect our family turned out, we are equally perfect in our own way. After all, are we not created in God's image, as the bible says? If we missed the mark on a few points of key doctrine, in our hearts we are exactly the good Christians he wanted us to be. We're kind, loving people, sensitive to others. If we each of us have made our mistakes, we did what we thought was right at the time. If we've failed each other, in words or in actions, then love and forgiveness is the only way forward.

∼

When I first got news of my father's stroke, a part of me felt relieved; now I could stay home where it's comfortable. It gave me a credible excuse to drop everything I was doing and put my energy elsewhere, which was the whole point of the Australian scheme anyway. And yet my instincts told me it wasn't the right thing to do. It's not as though I left him alone; he's got a better support system than most people I know. His new home is just a few blocks from my mother's and he has three children, two daughters-in-law, and a batch of grandkids in close vicinity. He'll be just fine.

Whichever way you swing it, I left for myself in the end. I'm not sure what kind of a person that makes me or if I should even be ashamed to admit such things. When it comes down to the wire, you just have to do what your heart tells you to do. My heart was telling me I had to go. I'm not a wanderer by nature, but neither do I run away from what scares me. Something in me was pushing hard to get out of there, away from the familiar, to plunge headfirst into the unknown.

It's possible I'm seeking to justify something I'm still a bit uneasy about, but I had to go with my gut on this one. I believe that our first duty in life is to find joy; only then can you go spreading it around to others. Eventually I would come to understand that you don't go *looking* for joy, the same way you can't go *looking* for peace. You just decide to feel it and then put all your energy into that. The justification of those feelings has nothing to do with geography; you seek the justification in the otherwise unremarkable, by expressing gratitude for the minutiae of your daily life. But then I had to cross the ocean to figure that out.

Hello, Yellow Brick Road

It defies all logic that someone with seven years of university education should be handing out samples in the supermarket. I'm pretty sure that the fifteen-year-old kids who round up the shopping trolleys and wheel them back into the store make more money than I was. What I have learned is that a three-quarters-completed Bachelor of Laws doesn't actually get you very far in the professional world, as many people were kind enough to point out before I left. The irony is that a completed Bachelor of Laws doesn't get you anywhere either. You can't practice law or for that matter even work as a legal secretary; there's a whole separate diploma program for that. If you're lucky, you might get $250/week as a legal intern but only if you are attending Bar School in the evening.

The degree that I did finish was a Bachelor of Fine Arts, another big winner in the world of high-flying professionals. Despite what one might think, being able to recite the first sixteen chords of Charlie Parker's *Ornithology* isn't a highly sought after skill in terms of employability. It does, however, make for a creative job hunter, one who is not afraid to style herself as master-in-training of a dozen different trades.

With an eternally dwindling pool of piano students (they're notoriously fickle), I endeavour to subsidise my teaching hours with a few French students. After all, I lived in Quebec for almost a decade. In Australia, that makes me practically French-Canadian, might as well market myself as one.

And so it was that Frosty came into my life. Frosty's wife, Pauline, had advertised in an online classified that her husband was seeking a French teacher and hired me almost on the spot after I responded to her ad, which speaks more to the lack of French speakers in Hervey Bay than it does to my skills as a teacher.

Pauline and Frosty are in their sixties. Although they live twenty minutes away, Frosty likes driving into the "city" to visit his young language teacher. He arrives every other morning and presents Juli and me with a fresh packet of Tim-Tams, a sort of Australian take on the Oreo. The entirety of our first two weeks is spent drinking coffee and learning things like, *"veux-tu un autre café"* and *"combien de sucres tu veux que je mette la-dans?"* When it becomes clear he will spend the entire hour regaling me in English with stories of his life in Africa, Frosty extends his lessons to two hours daily.

In less than a month Frosty will return to West Africa, where he works eight months a year for a mining company. Like my sister, Pauline is on her own for most of the year. In the seventies when Frosty first went to work in Africa, they were allowed one minute per week to speak on the sat-phone. In broken French, he tells me about the time they wasted their weekly sixty-seconds in a bitter dispute. In the week between calls, Frosty had blown up the argument to elephantine proportions; cursing Pauline for her imaginary rebuttals to such an extent he had himself convinced it was the end of his marriage. Meanwhile Pauline had completely forgotten the source of their disagreement and gone about business as usual.

We never quite get to the end of the story since Frosty's narratives have the habit of fading one into the other and the mix of languages make them that much more difficult to follow. But I think the lesson my student is attempting to teach me is never to end a conversation in anger, you'll only waste a lot of time feeling bad when you could be feeling good. I pass this information on to my sister, for whom I believe the story was intended, and resolve not to waste any more time re-analyzing a series of humdrum communiqués from César still sitting in my inbox.

A few days before Frosty is to depart for Africa, he and Pauline invite Juli and me for a farewell BBQ at their country house. Frosty calls it a "geriatric barbeque" but explains they like to let loose and he can give us the number of a Dial-a-Driver service should the drinking get out of hand. Juli and I chop a platter of vegetables for the party and plan to be home by 9:00 p.m., without the aid of any car services. Frosty, on the other hand, is mercilessly attentive from the moment we walk in the door, topping up our drinks every quarter of an hour until we're half in the bag before the appetizers have even been served.

His geriatric chums are an eclectic mix of Australians, South Africans, English gentlemen and their wives. They make wildly inappropriate jokes at the dinner table, slopping whisky and cokes all over the place, yelling and swearing like teenagers. At least three times Frosty rises to his feet and makes an elaborate scene of toasting his French teacher until I am blushing like crazy, drunk and making wild speeches about how happy I am to be dining at their table on the other side of the world.

I'm smiling so hard my face hurts, trying to take a mental snapshot and make this moment last forever. For the first time, the feeling hits me that I am falling in love with Australia and I savour these few seconds of fearlessness, freedom from anxiety, and pure love. Music from the twenties is playing on the radio until someone makes a comment that the singer sounds like he is having a prostate exam and so Frosty puts on Dance Mix '95. From there, everything sort of fades to black. Juli and I are recovering for two days; we loath to admit that we can hardly keep up with a bunch of senior citizens.

~

Sunday night, well into a second bottle of wine, I abruptly declare that I will play at every venue in town! In the morning, I begin reinventing myself as a lounge singer. In lieu of a suitable promotional photo, I dig through my hard drive and come up with a photo of a musician friend playing the piano, arm reaching elegantly across the keyboard, face turned away from her microphone, looking more graceful than a ballerina. Before any faulty wiring can convince me of the irrationality of such actions, I email every venue in Hervey Bay and attach this photo, making a mental note to try and imitate this gesture at every performance.

Hervey Bay is extremely courteous with me, which is ironic for a country where political incorrectness is so commonplace. Each and every proposal, no matter how poorly composed, is promptly and politely responded to within twenty-four hours. What is even more bewildering is that people are interested; within two days I have three weekly gigs lined up; I set about negotiating a handful of Christmas parties and special events. Having sent out my inquiries on a wing and a prayer, I use the same method to determine my value as a lounge performer, $125/45min, and no one but me balks at the absurdity of such a sum.

As October creeps in with the blistering hot Australian sun, Canada begins to fade into the background. I put the grocery stores and sample counters firmly in the past. I have an overwhelming feeling of redemption; this is the recognition I've been waiting for my whole life. Such is this unexpected boost in my earning potential that I stumble into bed at 8:30 p.m., exhausted from all the excitement, but it takes yogic concentration to stay asleep for more than a few hours. I lay awake at night mentally paying off debts and contemplating tax evasion strategies.

My eyes snap open at 5:00 a.m., even on Sundays. I am jerked into a state of alertness when it suddenly occurs to me, I don't have a booking agent in Dubai! I've got to book a month-long repos in Koh Chang for the New Year so I can meet up with friends in Angkor Wat in early February. By 6:00 a.m., I am at my computer researching which Vegas hotels have a piano in the lobby or which cruise ships pay the highest rates to their entertainment. By 7:00 a.m., I am convinced I'll be hired without any qualifications as star foreign music teacher at a fancy Catholic private school down the road. I'll have my debts paid off by June at which point I'll head out on the prawn trawlers and come back wealthier than King Tut. By August I will be lighting Cubans with hundred dollar bills.

The sense of urgency is more than a little overwhelming and so it comes as a relief when a law firm offers me some temporary work preparing a trial. All the dreaming is running me ragged. In a parallel universe, a law firm seems like exactly the right place to get some rest and recharge my batteries. The litigator I am working for assigns me my very own office, which makes me feel very professional and important, and it's very satisfying to settle in with some good old-fashioned paperwork. Even with all the hypothetical gigs coming in I haven't actually seen any money yet, though I've spent a fair bit outfitting myself for the job and I can sense my sister is irritated such sums were not allotted to more immediate needs like grocery bills, beer, and sunblock.

~

Very unexpectedly I start missing home so much it hurts. I write letters to my friends, my parents, even my former would-be in-laws, parents of the elusive Jean-Marc. I miss everyone so badly I can feel my heart beating in my chest. I miss people I don't even like. I miss my life in Montreal: the bitchy left-wing hippies from school and the smug metrosexuals who are always breaking my heart, Poutine Galvaude, Francophones, main street loft parties, cold weather, calling my mother four times a day, checking if anyone wrote about me on *missed encounters*, illegal consumption of alcohol in the architecture park. Each morning after my sister leaves for the Boat Club I curl up into a ball and imagine I am back home sprawled out on the sofa, Suggies the cat purring at my feet, autumn leaves blowing around outside my window.

The seasons are all turned around now. Rather than decompressing as one does in November in Canada, life is exploding all over. Summer is coming. Fat grapefruits are falling off the trees and brightly coloured birds are singing at all hours. Flowers are blooming. I'm supposed to be doing that too.

Someone once told me there's a lull in long-term travel that occurs sometime after the first few weeks. You get lethargic, dejected and sad for no reason. That must be this. Just last week I suddenly went man-crazy and couldn't understand what was pushing me to ask strangers if they had any single, thirty-something sons. I even asked Juli's husband to bring down some of his fishing mates from the north. In the end I suppose I am just looking for some comfort, which is ironic because I can't imagine anything more comfortable than here and now. If you asked me to describe comfort, it would be this: lying here on the beach with my sister in this sunny southern hemisphere.

~

Life can change so quickly, often when you least expect it. One minute you are wrapped up in the foetal position and longing for home, then next you are cruising down the highway in a campervan, hair whipping around in the wind, sharing a hand-rolled cigarette with your German lover.

Three backpackers install themselves down the road from our house in a couple of illegally parked campervans. Their vans are freedom on wheels; mattress and frame bolted into the body, clothing, toiletries, and kite boards stowed away underneath. It's the ultimate kid's clubhouse, a fort for grown-ups. Instead of temporary walls fashioned with pillows and blankets, it has a fully functioning kitchen, a 2x3ft living room, and a comfortable sleeping area for two. From the passenger seat, the whole world looks different again. Canada sinks back into the background.

If Australia didn't invent the backpacker, it gave the idea form and meaning. It's the country that installed barbeques, beachside showers and (somewhat) clean toilets in hundreds of small towns along twenty-five thousand kilometres of coastline. Its farmers count on the yearly influx of backpackers to pick their bananas, avocados, and rockmelons, anything ripe for the reaping. They're paid well to do the jobs that ordinary Australians are unwilling to do themselves. Anyone under thirty is welcome to a working holiday visa, which is easily renewable with the right amount of regional labour under your belt.

It's always sunny somewhere in Australia so backpackers travel around the coast with the seasons, following the sunshine. Even with the sharks and the crocodiles, there's almost always a good place for an afternoon swim or at the very least a stroll on the beach. If you don't happen to have a campervan, there are hostels a-plenty for as little as $15/night. Some will even pick you up from the airport. Big grocery chains are not shy about sharing their day-olds with strays; while backpackers themselves are so shameless about bin diving it's practically a rite of passage.

These are the sorts of things I learn from our neighbours on wheels, whom we met during an uncharacteristic drinking blitz at the local Irish pub. They shame me for drinking *XXXX Gold* (the pride of Queensland, in my defence) and introduce me to *Toohey's Extra Dry*, a somewhat more sophisticated brew and the pride of New South Wales, which we drink on the beach until sunset while barbequing kangaroo in the moonlit park. Wading into the water after dark, my hands gripping my skirt, I wonder what more there is to life than this.

Amongst the campers I resolve to take a lover, a German who owns one of the vans, lives to get stoned and eat four-deck Nutella sandwiches. If we're being honest, Klaus is more interested in my sister than me, but these are the sorts of things you stop caring about when you come to Australia. Choosing a lover is a bit like choosing between *XXXX Gold* and *Toohey's Extra Dry* – important, sure, but not worth considering too much. They come and go and so do you. That's the way it works in paradise.

Long after their campervans have disappeared down the coast, their spirit of adventure lingers on. Maybe it's the kangaroo meat or maybe it's the summer really coming on full force, but I have a sudden urge to move that's stronger than any I can remember. In all honesty, I didn't really come to Australia for Australia. I came to get away from where I was rather than any real desire to get where I was going. More than anything I came for my sister, who's been absent far too long. With its colourful characters and sandy beaches, Australia has won my heart. Now that I've had a sip of it, I want to gulp it down.

So I've made the decision to bounce and soon. When the big dough comes through, which I feel certain it will, I'll get myself a station wagon, an old mattress, and a butane camp stove. I'll play every bar, club, and hotel lobby in the country and sleep in parking lots if I have to. Each day will be more thrilling than the last. I'll shower on the side of the road and camp for weeks in the caravan parks of Australia. I'll subsist on the dirt and sand, drink *Lift* and snack on *kanga bangers* when I get really hungry. I'll fall in love a million times until my heart is tough as leather. By the time I make it to Ayer's Rock, I'll have grown a pair of wings the span of which is so wide you can spot them from the moon. When I'm swooping down across Uluru, I'll know I've made it.

~

I book a five-day engagement, at four hundred dollars a night, on Daydream Island and become convinced this is the universe conspiring with me in the call to action. This is the break I've been waiting for, a chance to run wild and really suck the juice from life. Never mind that I was supposed to go back to Canada at the end of December, who could refuse a paid holiday in a place called Daydream Island? I can't think of a better Christmas gift then the sand, sun, and tropical beaches of the Great Barrier Reef. You'd have to be crazy to turn it down. I've done crazy before but not that kind of crazy.

As it turns out, no one expected me home for Christmas anyway. My friends had already predicted I would travel, find a job, maybe fall in love with a man, with Australia, or both. Back in Canada I'd have laughed and scoffed at such suggestions. I'm not a fly-by-the-seat-of-your-pants kind of woman. I'm a strategiser and an executioner of plans. And yet Australia has made an adventurer out of me, as it has done of many before. Australia took my suffocated, lawyering heart and prised it open with dingoes and palm trees and tropical birds and breathed fresh air into its withering cavities. I wouldn't say I don't care about all that stuff anymore, but it's moved down a whole lot of rungs on my ladder of priorities.

~

Once my German lover and his campervan comrades are gone, the memories of crisp summer nights spent pressed up against each other under the glow of the moon begin to fade and I suddenly feel heartbroken again. That's the problem with falling in love all the time; someone is always breaking your heart. The way I see it, I've got two choices; I can either teach my heart never to love again or I can head up north for some fruit picking and try to make it a triple-header. It's early November. Most of my lounge-singing work won't get rolling for at least another month, so the logical thing to do in the meantime is earn some extra cash on the farms of Bundaberg, only an hour from Hervey Bay.

Full of hope and grab-the-bull-by-the-balls enthusiasm, I'm on the bus within days.

Bundaberg is an unqualified disaster. The hostel has an open-air deck bar that blares cheap dance music and flashes fluorescent lights until 3:00 a.m. I'm probably the only person here who is over the age of twenty-two; I'm also the only person who seems concerned about it. Worse, there's hardly any work this month since the rains have been slow to arrive this season. When I reluctantly admit that I am unwilling to commit to a full month's work, the hostel flatly refuses to refer me for any farm work in the area.

In the morning I'm up at 6:00 a.m. with my bags packed. If this is adventure, I want no part of it. The first bus doesn't arrive until the afternoon so I plod out to the now-quiet deck bar and drown my sad heart in celery and onion dip, which is the only food I brought along and I haven't got the spirits to waste any more money on this misguided escapade in Bundaberg. In between withered celery sticks I befriend a travelling Irishman, who is also not twenty-two, and who agrees to while away a few hours drinking milky tea at McDonalds on his dime, a real cultural foray for the both of us. Sadly he does not break my heart, but still I leave full of hope and excitement for all of my past and future loves.

Loserville

Life as a professional musician is truly no picnic. Every day brings fresh rejection. The offers are so big and the stakes so high, it's impossible not to feel despair when the bulk of my grand plans fall flat. Even the dream of a rickety station wagon is fading fast. Three months into my trip, my bank account continues to plummet further and further until I am mostly living on credit. Even Juli begins to lose patience. She leaves the house early, pulling split shifts five days a week, and is understandably irritated coming home to find her jobless other half sprawled on the couch with a belly full of wine.

Each day I twist my stomach into a ferocious knot phoning club owners, booking agents, hotels, and restaurants trying to hustle up some work. My leads from early October refuse to gel into anything concrete. The line between asking for work and begging for work gets fuzzier and fuzzier until it becomes impossible to tell which side I am on. I sense they can smell my desperation. When a booker suddenly has to take an important call or is inexplicably out of the office for days at a time, the wheels in my head begin to turn. I'm *that* girl; the girl you go on one date with and then have to continuously dump day after day when she refuses to get the message.

The highs are so very high and the lows so very low. One afternoon I ferry out to Fraser Island, where I am playing on a grand piano in a pseudo-log-cabin-style resort with 40-foot ceilings, allowing myself to be romanced between sets by a wealthy Irishman and gulping down all the complimentary merlot I can handle. The next I'm back at the Boat Club, sandwiched in a corner behind a large, overbearing Christmas display, an enormous banner hanging in front of my face announcing a holiday raffle, playing overtop the house music that the night manager has forgotten to shut off.

The insults pile on, deflating my ego a little more every time. Daydream Island backs out, citing opposition from the higher-ups. Another island resort rings up raving about my talent over the phone but then avoids my phone calls for weeks. After a nerve wracking audition before a jury of three Aussie hoteliers, their in-house restaurant hires me two nights a week and then delays my start date again and again, claiming problems with permits and regulations prevent them booking a date. A bar in the bay promises work from week to week but never seems to have enough bookings to justify live entertainment. The local RSL club is beside themselves with applause and books me for two nights a week, even proposing a full-out photo shoot and advertising campaign. After two months, countless emails and dozens of unreturned phone calls, the marketing manager finally picks up the phone, tells me what a sweet doll I am and assures me he will call back in a fortnight, which of course he doesn't.

I train at the piano for hours a day until I am obliged to spend half my weekly wages on physiotherapy to heal my aching tendons. In sympathy, the divine universe throws me a bone in the form of a young Aussie, Mark, who runs the car rental shop down the road. The Aussie copied my number down from the waiver I had signed in his shop, an act I cannot imagine being performed in any civilized country but Australia. Though he is decidedly unattractive to me and often drunk when we meet, I can't help but be charmed by his plain disregard for business ethics. So of course I say yes when he asks me for drinks at the beach.

Mark brings over boxes of beers and prattles on for hours, taking my mind off the burning loneliness and crushing disappointments. He massages my shoulders like a professional masseur and leaves miracle muscle relaxers in our mailbox. He carts me all over town at the slightest provocation and then cheerfully buggers off when I need a night alone. And when I need a night not alone, he comes over in his truck and drives me back to his place to eat chips and watch nature shows. We mostly sit in silence and pretend to be a real couple, though it is obvious to us both that we are not.

Strange as it sounds, young Mark really does provide some comfort — even more so in retrospect. A few weeks in he abruptly calls an end to our little faux-mance, announcing he has decided to give it a final go with his former sweetheart. I endorse this plan wholeheartedly and give him my good wishes and blessings. My heart feels just a faint twinge of regret at another ending having come just a little bit too soon.

The final insult is when the Boat Club, my weekly and now only gig, cancels my four final performances: "Monday night piano entertainment is not of a standard that is required to achieve the goal of entertaining and keeping patrons in the club longer," they say. Yikes. Luckily my ego has been unequivocally shot for weeks already. After much finagling and loosely disguised threats of legal action, they agree to bring me back for a final two performances.

Strolling back into the club that fired me for lack of talent and attempting to entertain the crowd for two hours is very sobering. The cheap, cordless microphone is once again out of batteries and I have to keep calling the manager over to bring new ones. Every time I hit a wrong note I wince and scrunch up my face like a child, which is how I feel — like a child putting on a show for her indulgent parents, who applaud politely even as they are silently lamenting their poor, talentless offspring.

The Boat Club has been a sort of home for me. Patrick the security guard is as friendly an overseas father figure as you could wish for. Steve the bus driver has never once reported me for taking the patrons-only courtesy bus to and from work for twelve weeks straight. Ron the duty manager likes to go on for hours about his love affair with Canada. Rob the bartender is always waiting with a rum and ginger beer. I even feel something for the Keno attendant who never recognises me even though I've been picking up my cheque at his desk every week for three months. I even spent my first Melbourne Cup here, shamelessly boozing and flirting at two in the afternoon on a Tuesday with four (gasp) married men, betting and losing what was left of my pathetic salary on the famed annual horse race. It is impossible to feel sour about the Boat Club. It hurts bad, but sometimes it hurts so good.

~

As if to highlight the spectacular proportions of my failures, my sister's husband returns from his latest trawling excursion and moves back into the house to serve as a secondary witness. I move my things out of the guest room and into the downstairs bedroom at the back of the house, where I can lay around whimpering like an unemployed loser and feel sorry for myself without interruption. As the temperature rises, the days feel longer. I continue to learn new material and pepper club owners with phone calls but it's plain to see my heart is no longer in it.

With Captain Sparrow back home, the tension in the house is briefly lifted. My sister is thrilled to have her husband home and get back to the business of procreation, which they've been working at for some time now. While Juli works, Sparrow and I spend our days sprawled out on the back porch hiding from the blistering November sun, which is now penetrating every corner of the house. Sparrow throws himself into the search for a suitable fishing boat. I linger in front of my computer pretending to work.

I'm not working though, and the guilt is growing exponentially with each passing day. Sparrow doesn't seem concerned about my lack of contribution, though it is my sister who manages their finances and he is hardly *au courant*. She never says so explicitly but I can tell she's had just about enough of her freeloading housemate. She thinks about money a lot; easy for me to say when I'm not paying the bills. But I can tell it's on her mind almost every minute of the day. She's my sister after all and we've been thick as thieves since we were babies. I know what goes on in head.

To make matters worse, since Sparrow got back from the sea he's been burning through their savings like a glutton pouring gravy all over his turkey dinner. Since he spends two thirds of the year at sea, he feels justified in spending his hard-won earnings on a bit of R&R. This is his time to let loose and enjoy the good life. Yet you can hardly fault his wife her frustration when she heads out for her second shift of the day just as her husband and sister are digging into yet another case of *XXXX Gold*.

My sister cleans to alleviate her frustration, though it hardly seems to help. I can tell she's upset with us when she clears off the counter completely, sprays it down with a bottle of antibacterial something-or-other, and starts wiping compulsively at every surface in the house. She's maniacal in her commitment to the task, refusing help on principle. It's possible the cleaning is meant to underline our laziness but I don't think she is consciously aware of it.

Sparrow and I burn through cases of beer almost daily, lounging on the back porch from sunup 'til sundown. We hardly know each other and the conversation is stifled. This makes us want to drink more, naturally, and we do. Eventually he buys his boat and the three of us motor around on the Fraser Coast a few times a week. The warm salty air and secluded white beaches do wonders, buoying our spirits and wiping away some of the awkwardness that's been growing in the house like mould, soiling the surfaces of our daily exchanges.

Even with the sand and sun and the thrill of the open water, the tension continues to mount. Sparrow and I laze about like a couple of languid sea creatures and Juli is more and more grateful for her work since it at least gets her out of the house five days a week. I start looking for work out of town, not seriously at first, but at least this way no one can accuse me of dragging my heels.

Accusations are shot through the house like invisible bullets, everyone feeling simultaneously irrational and justified. My sister and her husband argue frequently and though it's awkward to witness, I'm secretly grateful to have the attention directed away from me. With Sparrow's incessant drinking and Juli's all-consuming desire for babies, there is an enormous fault line cracking open between them, one that seems impossibly wide, across which my sister has more and more difficulty conjuring imaginary bridges.

Every sign is pointing to the nearest exits. The pressure is mounting to near combustion levels and I've got to get out before it blows the roof clean off. It is both exhilarating and intensely saddening to see the end of my time in Hervey Bay. I'm only sorry that it's coming to completion on a low note. Someday I will rewrite this time in my memory and gloss it over with the sheen of nostalgia. I can almost feel how that will go already.

Though I didn't manage to improve myself financially or professionally, the last few months have changed me. I was such a hopeless mess when I arrived, a sad bird limping away from the big tree I'd fallen out of. With all her frustrations and imperfections, my sister helped me sew together my broken wings. She welcomed me into her home and took care of me. The next time I fall from a tree my bones will be stronger; they will not crack so easily.

Despite the growing list of catastrophes and disappointments, I did accomplish something big here: I've commenced a seismic shift. Everything is different now. Life can never be the same again.

Apotheosis

Looking back on my life in Canada gives me a choking feeling in my chest. Something was buried there that is itching to be dug up. But the thing is so deep, my shovel is small and each mound of dirt will need to be held up to the light and carefully scrutinized before I can toss it into the sand pile of memory. So much light and so much darkness, so much sour taste in my mouth. Even if the hangover has long begun to subside, some sharp, acidic bile lingering in the back of my throat creeps out when I least expect it. Even though my heart does a savage sort of beating when it brings up that dark matter, the time has come to burn down the remains of that crumbling castle, soak in a bath of its ashes, and be born anew.

~

Three years ago I enrolled in law school at Université du Québec à Montréal as a kind of experiment. I taught piano lessons part-time, studied part-time and took out a loan to pay for my tuition and books. I moved to an impoverished neighbourhood in Montreal where I could live on a thousand dollars a month. Most of my neighbours were on the dole. Many had dogs that lived indoors and barked loudly far into the night. The street entrance led you up a wrought iron spiral staircase that opened into the murky corridor

I shared with the apartment next door. The teenagers with whom this glamorous entryway was divided sold drugs to pay the rent and generously waited two months before robbing me blind one afternoon when I had briefly slipped out to see my therapist, leaving the back door unlocked. Still I took an enormous amount of pride in poverty and self-sacrifice, even more so after my neighbours stripped me of every item of value I owned. I was just grateful to have been robbed in the summertime and not during exam season when no amount of money could replace hours of laborious paper writing I never thought to back up.

In those days I was still feeling my way around in a world entirely new; a world of native French speakers who cared about things like lawyering. Most of my friends were English speaking, slept until noon, played at least one instrument and only worked when absolutely necessary. For me, that was Montreal. Living an artist's life gave me definition. I relished my status as the lone Anglophone, Ontarian girl at a French school in a sea of militant, flag-waving Francophones. The university was purportedly pushing a socialist agenda, having been founded as the law school of the people and an alternative to the upper class, English-speaking tyranny of the two other more internationally recognised law schools in Montreal. I imagined that I would fit in in such a place.

The reality was quite different. Most of the students were just as corporate minded as any other law school. Most of them went there because they didn't get in anywhere else, though we persisted in the "social-good" charade. Competition was just as fierce; students compared grades obsessively, shared notes selectively, and formed their own invite-only study groups.

Back then my French was lamentable at best. I could hardly string together a sentence, let alone claw my way into one of these ghastly cliques. To the best of my abilities and with the aid of my peripheral vision, I would choose a seat next to anyone with mild manners and semi-decent handwriting and shamelessly copy their notes while trying in vain to follow the lecture, which was all French all the time. Eventually I worked up the nerve to bat my eyes wildly at one of the younger male students and ask if he would email me the notes I'd been watching him take on his laptop. To his credit (and that of law students in general), he took pity on me and obliged. Even though he spent a good portion of class looking at muscle cars on the Internet, I was still exceedingly grateful for the insights his lectures notes afforded me and considered myself lucky to have something resembling a friend in my constitutional law class.

My objective that first year was just to pass the classes and improve my French, which I did, although by then it was clear that wouldn't get me far in the legal world. The best internships, nay, any internships, inevitably went to the students with the highest grades and the best command of the language, both written and spoken. Early on I'd have said I didn't give a damn about all that; this was just an experiment, after all. But it didn't take long to get reeled in by the *Bitch-Goddess of Success*.

Somewhere along the line things got serious. I started attending law firm cocktails and seminars on how to interview in legalese. I wore trendy pantsuits and interviewed for boring summer internships in dull offices in equally dull skyscrapers. Struggling to express myself articulately in French, I inevitably came off as slightly dim-witted or slow, clearly not cut out for a cutthroat career in lawyering. No matter how boring and ordinary I portrayed myself to be, I could never quite hide the fact that I was an outsider, a misfit, an English-Canadian piano player disguised as a law student.

~

In their second year, many of my fellow students began sporting their business suits in class. Presumably some of them had jobs by then and were hauling themselves back and forth from work to school. Perhaps they hadn't the time to change into their human clothes with all the shuttling around but more likely they were just eager to distinguish themselves as belonging to the elite squad of employed law students. Others were so hungry for the nine-to-five, so impatient for a life of dressing in shades of grey, that they were merely getting a jump-start on a life of mundanity. My colourful headscarves and loud gold brooches only served as a confirmation of my status as a curiosity, a strange, inexplicable presence amongst the more conservative, suit-wearing majority. I made two friends, one of whom I lost in a bitter competition for a seemingly coveted (if glaringly insignificant in retrospect) summer position at the public library, and another who remains my friend today, one with whom I could frantically eat, smoke, and drink to excess and bitch about law school — a kindred spirit.

Law school is a pressure cooker. Most courses are evaluated by way of two exams, one of which is held midway through the session and another at the end. Each one is long and painful, requiring hours and hours over textbooks, actively participating in study groups, and combing through previous years' exams. Even then there is almost always a good portion of students who fail and are subsequently obliged to drop the class. If your skin is thick enough to survive three years of writing five such exams twice per session, hopefully you are also lucky enough to have access to approximately ten thousand dollars, the entirety of which you will have to use to attend Bar School, the obligatory next step — a tidy sum to spend on eight months of additional torture for which the success rate is a cool fifty percent. And even after all this you are faced with the very real possibility of spending months or even years searching for the articling position you will need to complete your training and be officially called to the Bar. There are far fewer articles than there are law students and firms know this. In Montreal, many firms offer gruelling articles that demand an enormous number of hours and pay less that $250/week – cruel punishment indeed.

So why do it? Maybe when you invest so much energy in something so extraordinarily challenging and somehow miraculously endure a whole year without getting knocked over, you think, maybe I can do another. So you do one more and even though you feel like a human punching bag at the end of two years, you start to think, well, this can't all be for nothing, might as well do one more. And so it goes.

∼

Year three dropped on my head like an anvil. My grades, which until then had been subpar but not embarrassingly so, began to plummet with a vengeance. For the first time, I failed an exam so badly that I was advised to drop the class since it would take more than a miracle to bounce back. Rather than feeling like a noteworthy, non-conformist, alternative-type, I looked at myself in the mirror one day and saw a worthless failure of a law student staring back at me. In the mornings I would wake up, open my books and cry. In the afternoons I would gather myself together and drag my tired body to class, willing myself not to turn around. At break time it took a heroic effort not to ditch my coat and book bag and run, run, run, as fast as I could away from there. But then I would think of my mother, our social circle, and all the people I imagined would be let down if I couldn't see this thing through 'til the end.

Law school became the ultimate strength of character test. My ability to succeed would define me as a determined and capable person. Even more, it would define me to the world as a *somebody*. If I couldn't do this, where would that leave me? An unemployable dropout with seven years of university education and nothing to show for it. So I attended my lectures like a good girl, sneaking off to cry in the bathroom at break time when the going got really tough.

In hindsight, that was probably the beginning of the end. One morning midway into the fall semester of my third year, I ditched my books for a quick coffee run to the café round the corner. Hearing my stomach growl hungrily, I realised I'd missed breakfast and it was well past lunchtime. In a sudden moment of what I then perceived as divine inspiration, I decided to skip both meals and drink more coffee instead. I felt better instantly. Now here was something I could control. No amount of studying would earn me a passing grade in my Civil Obligations class or get me through law school inside of three years but surely losing five or ten pounds was the natural solution to my flailing ego. A lovely, trim body might just make up for the fact that, professionally and academically, I was an irredeemable loser. The more I thought about it, the better I felt. I resolved to eat cabbage salad for dinner and maybe skip breakfast again tomorrow. Why not get a jump-start on my new program?

And so it began. Skipping breakfast and lunch one morning became skipping breakfast and lunch for a week. Skipping breakfast and lunch for a week became eating nothing but lettuce and chia seeds for an entire month. I found a computer program that would allow me to track every item of food I ate in a day and compare it against all the calories I was burning through exercise and daily activities. I began spending less and less time in my textbooks and more and more time at the computer devising creative three hundred calorie meals. Though my aim was to ingest five hundred calories a day, I rarely achieved this appalling goal and would often sink into verbal abuse on days when I went over a thousand, which was not such an uncommon event. I berated myself further for failing even at anorexia. That feeling of regaining control quickly deserted me and was replaced with a heavy cloud of self-loathing.

Still I soldiered on. I kept up my studying, attended classes most of the time and, as a reward, splurged on a bathroom scale and began weighing myself several times a day. Losing five pounds didn't quite achieve the desired result so I told myself to lose five more and when that didn't work, I vowed to lose another five. Starvation was a kind of apotheosis for me, a way of reinstating some measure of control over the uncertainty and the mess I had made of myself. The reality is that I was anything but in control. In class, I was so hungry my head was spinning. Even if I'd had the presence of mind to take notes, I was far too busy with my calculations, deciding whether or not I could justify three chocolate covered almonds from the 25¢ machines in the cafeteria at break time. I started doing aerobics in my kitchen, two and then three times a day, all the while taking more painstaking notes on calories in and calories out.

More often than not, hunger got the better of me. On the way home from school I would stop at the grocery store and eat a whole box of sticky chocolate chip cookies in the drizzling snow before I even made it the four and a half blocks back to my apartment. Back home, I would feast on salty, highly flavoured foods, boxes of Kraft Dinner and bags of Doritos, telling myself

I deserved the ensuing sickness. Afterward I would vomit until my throat was so scratchy and dry I could hardly talk, which was perhaps to my benefit since the words I was speaking to myself were unthinkably cruel and unforgiving.

~

It's shocking the way you can become something you never imagined possible. You think you are a wolf until one day you wake up to find that somehow you are actually a lamb. As for me, I was a butterfly that one day found herself turned to a spider, to a creepy, ugly, unrecognisable thing. Somewhere in my subconscious, I'd rationalised that if I looked like on the outside what I was feeling on the inside, people would know how badly I was suffering and they would let me off the hook. If I was visibly sick, no one could fault me for quitting school. Every morning I would stand sideways in front of the mirror, hunch over my shoulders and suck my stomach in toward my arched back, to see how sickly I could make my ribcage appear. Contorting my body at odd angles and looking for the most unsightly protruding bones, I made my body into the image of my heart: shrunken and dry.

Amazingly, that semester I passed three out of four classes and shuffled home for the holidays. Christmas time was tricky. The loss of fifteen pounds on my already slight frame was probably alarming but perhaps not disturbingly so. If anyone made a comment, I would casually reply something about stress, the long hours of study or lack of time for food. I started lying and inventing excuses for skipping meals. Being among friends and family was uncomfortable and I hated myself even more for deceiving the people I loved most in the world. But even though my castle was visibly crumbling, I couldn't seem to find the strength to bulldoze it down. Lacking the courage to express myself verbally, I continued to do so physically.

The thinner I got, the harder it was to lose weight, forcing me to invent newer, more appalling methods. My partner, Jean-Marc, couldn't quite disguise how much he liked my thinness. Having transformed myself into his version of the feminine ideal, Jean-Marc would often compliment me on my lithe new body. I hated him for this and loathed him still more when he tried to touch the body for which I had paid such a high price. My body had become the physical expression of everything I hated about my life. In retrospect, the fact that Jean-Marc still found me attractive was probably a testament to how much he was suffering from a similar kind of self-loathing, disappointed as he was in what his own life had become.

There was no more laughter between us, no more tender looks, no more affection. Neither of us had anything left to give one another. A few weeks into the winter semester, Jean-Marc confessed he wanted a few weeks alone to "see if he could live without me." In a sort of apocalyptic climax, he eventually left me for good on the eve of my mid-term exams. I sobbed shamelessly and begged him not to go but Jean-Marc remained cold and unaffected. His mind was made up.

∼

Such was the nature of the hole I'd jumped into: Law School, a walk in the proverbial pit of fire except with tuition fees. Stripped of my last vestige of support, I eventually turned to the friends from whom I had been delicately concealing the sad state of affairs for months. And didn't they come through for me. They took me on spa dates and didn't ask too many questions. They invited me to dinners and never made any remarks about what or how little I ate. They called, visited, wrote encouraging emails at odd hours of the day. I found a therapist and slowly began my ascent back into the land of the living. My therapist, God bless her, stubbornly refused to give me permission to drop out of school. I was only a few weeks away from finishing anyway, and she must have known that somewhere I had strength to finish my third year. And so, little by little, I began to gather up the scattered fragments of my exploded heart and put the pieces back together. At the time recovery seemed protracted and slow, but looking back it's almost shocking how quickly everything came together again. Sometimes when you really let yourself hit the bottom you get a good hard surface to push off of. That's how it was for me, anyway.

In the end, nobody thought any less of me when I decided not to go back to school in the fall; they'd seen it coming a mile away. If anything they encouraged me to be free and run wild, at least for a little while. Not surprisingly, my mother never held it against me. Maybe one of the many lessons to be learned here is that no matter how badly we manage to fuck things up, regardless of the length of time or the depth with which we condescend to drag ourselves through the mud, it's pretty hard to shake a mother's love. Your friends support you because, well, that's what friends do. Your family forgives you because that's what families do.

People like to advise me about my future and I forgive them for it because, were they to face such trials themselves, I fancy they would probably know better, do better, or at the very least do things differently. If I made some bad choices, they only served to propel me to the place I am now, which is not such a bad place to be. I eat like a champion, four, sometimes five times a day. I am human again. When I make mistakes or do things badly, I can laugh at myself instead of punishing myself. People seem to like me, not because of my law degree or my grade point average but because, at the end of the day, I am not such a bad person to be around. I have a family that supports me and friends who would lie down on train tracks for me, a roof over my head and money in the bank. What more could I possibly ask for?

Leaving the Bay

It takes forty-seven minutes to cover the distance between the two piers on Scarness Beach. I know the precise measurement because I've been walking it almost every day in the weeks leading up to my departure. Since I am officially leaving now, having more or less thrown in the towel of my lounge-singing career, I have an unlimited amount of time for deliberation and contemplation, which sounds like an incredible luxury but in reality it is the bane of my beachside strolling. If I could get outside of myself, I might be able to enjoy the sound of the rolling waves or the gentle caress of the sun on my shoulder blades.

Now that summer is in full swing and the sun is ruthlessly punishing from 6:00 a.m. until sunset, most mornings I just frolic in the ocean and then pass the rest of the day on the couch, directly in front of the fan, cold beer in one hand and P.D. James in the other. I feel less guilty about it now that I am employed and try to recover some of my fallen grace by preparing elaborate meals and vacuuming the house while my sister works. It's a small contribution but if at least I am not remembered as "my lazy little sister who sat on the lounge for four months straight," I could be happy with that.

A resort in far north Queensland has hired me to wait tables and clean rooms, though I don't start until mid-December. That gives me just over two weeks to pace back and forth from pier to pier, waiting for the time to pass.

Leaving Hervey Bay is an exercise in letting go. Not just the jobs I didn't get, the men who dropped me, and the bills I never paid, but also the disappointed hopes and failed attempts at glory. I can't be bringing all that with me where I am going. This is a chance to leave all that behind and start fresh, again. Maybe being happy is like being in business; you have to go bankrupt a few times before you get it right. Bankruptcy can be a good thing; you start with a clean slate and build from the ground up, with the lessons you learned from your last enterprise but without all the overdue accounts and loose ends.

Leaving also means letting go of my sister — my rock and my teammate. Although our relationship has been strained over the last few weeks she is still my sister. In spite of it all, I think we did pretty well. We made mistakes along the way. If I had a do-over, I suppose I'd do some things differently but under the circumstances we did our best and we came out stronger and wiser. If neither of us shed tears at the airport it's only because we know we'll see each other again soon. We share the same geography, for now, which is more than I can say for the last half decade.

In a way, you're always letting go of something, of people who hurt you and plans that fell through, of employers who stiffed you or waitresses who forgot your drink orders. You can't be carrying the weight of all that everywhere you go, it's too heavy and it turns everything sour. With that in mind, Juli and I spend my last Sunday night in town at the local Church of Spirituality, where we are intent on opening our minds to a better future, free from the cares of yesterday. Incidentally, the evening meditation goes something like this:

In the Belly of Oz

You're standing on the beach listening to the gentle slosh-slosh of the waves. A cool breeze is blowing and, miraculously, you remembered to bring a warm shawl. You wade into the water to get a closer look at its impossible blue-green perfection and maybe to swat away a sand crab nipping at your toes. You notice a small boat, anchored in the shallow waters just a few feet away. You approach the boat and, finding it empty, you come to understand that this vessel is here for the express purpose of carrying away all your earthly and spiritual burdens. You proceed to unload your anxieties into the boat, one by one, until you feel blissfully relieved and refreshed. When you are finished, you take up the anchor, put it back in the boat and proceed to push the boat away from the shore.

As you wade waist deep into the water, you suddenly realise you are no longer afraid of sharks or poisonous jellyfish. You are completely consumed by your fear of letting go of the boat, you resist the urge to actually jump in the boat yourself and roll around in your own incorporeal filth for one precious moment or two. Maybe you actually do jump in. Maybe you reach in and pull out a last bit of emotional debris you are not willing to part with just yet. Walking back up the beach you are at once deliciously light and impossibly heavy. Gosh, your feet are so tired.

In an eleventh-hour-style act of desperation, you turn and run, back into the water and begin swimming desperately out to the boat, GIVE ME MY FOOLISHNESS BACK! Just as you are registering the rashness of this, your final act, you feel something clamp down on your right leg and you black out into perfect bliss as your earthly body is savagely devoured by crocodiles.

That's how it ended for me, anyway. In the official version the boat floated away without anyone coming to such a dramatic end. It's particularly hard to let go of personal failures. You can't help but wonder if you'd done something differently or played your hand all the way to the end that it might've turned out different. When do you know to quit and when do you know to keep plugging away? I can't seem to let go of this idea of being a *somebody*, can't stop obsessing about the attainment of this coveted status, even if I know it's a completely arbitrary and subjective measurement of success.

When you're young, intelligent and well educated you are expected to achieve great things. You are expected to contribute something significant to the world and also to make money doing it. Otherwise, you're bound to be listening for the rest of your life to a never-ending series of sermons about all the things you could've done and the wonders you might've accomplished, first from your parents and then from yourself. Before you know it you're lonely and underemployed, a character in a Billy Joel song — making love to your tonic and gin.

It's dreadful having all this *potential*; more of a curse than a blessing really, especially for women. In your late twenties, you're supposed to be establishing yourself professionally, getting all of that out of the way so you can get down to the more pressing business of childbearing, which is the only real vindication for lack of professional achievement. If you have children, you're off the hook.

At the same time, jobs are a lot like relationships in that you have to try a whole bunch before you get it right. You learn what you want and what you don't want and you gain skills you can take with you to the next one. It can take years to figure out you want nothing to do with the person or job in question. Hopefully your skills are easily translatable. If not, you have to start at the bottom again and work your way up the ladder.

~

The women of my family were not expected to do much professionally. In fact, very little was expected of the men either. We were not encouraged to pursue higher education or even to make the best grades. Most of us did anyway; we're a clever bunch. A much greater emphasis was placed on being the best Christians we could be. Applause would likely have been louder for marriage and subsequent babies than for degrees and high-powered careers. As it was, none of us were arriving at any of those milestones in the proper order, so marriages were mostly quiet affairs with little congratulatory fanfare on our father's part.

There were no shining examples of working women in our community. In the meetings we attended every Sunday, women were expected not to draw attention to themselves. It wasn't just pants that were frowned upon, it was also sleeveless shirts and anything else likely to attract male attention. Though the custom was not stressed, it was considered exemplary for women to wear head coverings at the very least to fellowship meetings, though she would be further applauded for donning such a style in her daily life as well.

Between my four brothers, my sister and I, only half of us graduated high school. Some of my brothers went on to work as tradesmen and so completed their GEDs and spent some time in college. My father operated a small painting and decorating business, so trades were a natural choice for his sons. It was thought proper for them to choose a career that would enable them to support a family, perhaps buy a house and a car. No one patted them on the back for such accomplishments or encouraged them one way or another. The work a man did during the day was nothing compared to the work he did at home, which was the most important work of all — that of ensuring the salvation of his earthly family.

As for my sister and I, it's difficult to know what exactly our father had hoped for us. Future plans were frowned upon in our family. It was not for us to decide the course of our lives; the Lord would direct our sails. I never once heard my father plan to do anything, without tacking on a cursory "Lord willing." Even on a quick trip to the grocery store, he'd say, "I'll be back in twenty minutes, Lord willing." I have heard this expression so often that the words are mashed together in my head — Lordwilling — as if it were all one word. *Lordwilling, we'll be there Sunday. I'm meeting him at five, Lordwilling.* You couldn't even plan to mow the lawn without questioning whether or not the Lord willed it so. It was as though the Lord might take offense to us making our own plans.

Since we refrained from discussing such earthly trivialities as careers, it was even less likely we would consider something as worldly as career *satisfaction*. The mere thought of it almost makes me shudder. Satisfaction was to be got from the Holy Spirit, from daily devotion and divine servitude. I was not well placed to be choosing a career with any particular thought or care. Even in the midst of my music degree, I had regular fits of unsatisfaction and would go about collecting pamphlets and applications forms from the engineering, mathematics and psychology departments, as though maybe there might be something better out there.

In truth I adored those four years. They were the magic university years you never get back; the ones that'll make your spouse grimace when you repeatedly refer to them as having been "the best of your life." Yet for some reason I dropped all thoughts of a musical career about five minutes after convocation, citing bitter competition and lack of talent. Law school was another colossal miscalculation. Suffice to say that I tried many things, succeeded at some and failed at a whole lot more. Although history abounds with characters whose careers went nowhere for decades, who found success far later in life, I'm determined to take comfort in the fact that I'm not alone.

Take Jesus, for example. So little is known about Jesus' youth that whole libraries of novels have been written in speculation of his mysterious adolescence and early adulthood. Notwithstanding one banal incident at temple, the bible is inexplicably mute on the subject of Christ's life before the age of 30. Presumably fed up with a low-paying career in carpentry (a métier he shared with Harrison Ford, also a late bloomer), he doesn't appear to have officially taken up his post as Son of God until after celebrating the big 3-0. What kind of shenanigans he got up to before is anyone's guess.

There's also my mother, Pashana the Great. Much like Jesus, my mother Pashana is called by many names. To my father, she is Kay. To her six children, she is Mom. To her clients, she is Lynda Kay Knapp, CFP. To many others, she is called teacher and to an enlightened few, she is Pashana. My mother was a professional homemaker for twenty-five years before wiping the slate clean and rebuilding her life. When she split with my father, her family and friends advised her to become a waitress. Nearly fifty, her primary skills were laundry and cooking. Surely waitressing was an obvious choice, what with my mother being already acquainted with a life of menial servitude.

But it wasn't the fifties anymore and my mother instinctively knew she had choices. She announced she would become a financial planner. People scoffed. They told her that she was not smart enough, that it would be decades before she enjoyed any measure of success. Her only supporter in this reckless endeavour was her slick-haired European boyfriend. And didn't she show them. Today Pashana is not only universally admired for her astounding spiritual and physical beauty but she is wildly successful in her career as a financial planner and gets more so with each passing year. Watching her tool around town in a gold Jaguar the size of a small submarine, she is most definitely a *somebody*.

Somewhat less remarkably, there is Martha Stewart. The patron saint of domesticity apparently intended to study chemistry and later the arts, finally graduating in European and architectural history. She married a lawyer, dabbled in modelling and ultimately settled into a career as a stockbroker. She eventually uncovered her talent for homemaking when remodelling her Connecticut farmhouse, which was the genesis of her career in the domestic arts. Her magazine, *Martha Stewart Living*, debuted in 1990, a year before her 50th birthday. She was still dabbling in stocks when she was convicted of insider trading at the age of sixty-one and sentenced to five months in the slammer. Apparently you are also never too old to be sent to prison.

Stan Lee was already in his 40's when he created Spiderman. Charles Bukowski worked in the post office for years before his first novel was published at the age of 49. Colonel Saunders didn't franchise KFC until he was 65. James Joyce worked as a singer and James Woods dropped out of MIT. Julia Child had her first cooking lesson at 36. Even Chairman Mao was a high school principle before he joined the Communist Party.

Obviously for a lot of people it takes a few extra years and a few false starts to really find a place in the world that is comfortable and somehow meets the expectation of what we thought our lives would be. To make matters still more complex, there are also an infinite number of variables on the job; the people you work with, the size of the company, the twenty-five shades of beige in your office. If you really get studying all the options and each of their variables, it starts to feel like one big game of cards.

The globalised world is all about choice, a paralyzing plethora of options big enough to make your head spin. I wonder if we are any happier than we were way back when. Maybe the secret is to just pick something and go with it. Statistically speaking, arranged marriages are just as likely to succeed as the ones we choose for ourselves. In a grocery store setting, studies show that the fewer the options, the more likely a person is to purchase a product. Companies pay big money to find the magic number when it comes to choices and the answer is never infinity. Often it's more like five or six.

When it comes to choices, less is undoubtedly more. So where does that leave the twenty- and thirty-somethings of the postmodern era who are endlessly bombarded with such choices? Many of us are fumbling in the dark, leaving things more or less to fate. The only thing that really makes any sense is to do something you love, something that inspires you, and bank on catching a break somewhere along the line. Otherwise you can dig into something really gritty that is known to get high returns, like lawyering.

There's a lesser-known third option I'm only just now getting acquainted with and that's travelling Australia hobo-style, flipping the proverbial bird to the money-grubbing modern world. With hardly more than the clothes on your back, you can make a pretty good life picking fruit for fast cash and snorkelling in the Great Barrier Reef on your downtime. You can drive from town to town, working at outback pubs and living on fresh-caught barramundi. As for myself, I'm determined to become the world's most well educated cleaning lady. In Australia, such waywardness is not just for tourists and rebellious dropouts; even Australians are doing it. Nobody is going hungry; the people sleeping on the beach are there by choice.

We have this idea that there is a price to pay in order to get somewhere. From a young age, we are taught that "paying one's dues" is an important rung on the ladder of success. So you slug it out at law school or resolve to put in five years in the mailroom of some dreary corporate basement. In all your suffering and self-sacrifice, you get to thinking that the end result must be something really important. That elusive promotion or pay-raise becomes your purpose. It's the justification for the years you spent in the proverbial mailroom and the longer you stay in that mailroom, the more necessary it becomes.

In the process of all this planning and career-mongering, it's easy to forget about joy. Joy is the only credible destination; if you're not getting there, you're getting nowhere. That's where the backpackers have got one up on the money-chasers. They're actively looking for joy, every day, prising it from the big open hands of this country. I'm not saying it's the only way to get to joy; there are a number of ways to do that. But when I get on that plane and officially join the wandering ranks of the youth of Australia, I'm going ahead with joy as my new system of measurement.

PART TWO

WEIPA, FAR NORTH QUEENSLAND

The Other Great North

Stepping off the plane in Cairns is like stepping inside a hot air balloon. The weather is so thick with humidity; it takes concerted effort to suck the oxygen from the congealed air. Inside the airport, the air-conditioning is turned up so high that I am cowering over my laptop in long pants, a thick cotton cardigan and a good, Canadian scarf even though it's forty degrees outside.

Welcome to northern Australia. I've taken a job at the Albatross Bay Hotel in Weipa, Queensland, a few hours north of Cairns, a few hours closer to the equator, a few hours deeper into the hot air balloon. I couldn't go back to Canada, couldn't stay where I was, couldn't go back to law school, couldn't sing one more Billy Joel song to a crowd of senior citizens who weren't listening anyway.

I found the job on the Internet. God Bless Australia — I made two phone calls and the matter was settled. It'll be real work this time, pulling pints, scrubbing toilets, the whole bit. No glamour. No accolades. Just hard work in exchange for hard cash. There's something oddly refreshing about it. I've been avoiding this for nine years. Studying, singing in bars, giving piano lessons. Now I'm going to do what normal people do: work. Maybe normal is what's been missing.

Five-hour layovers are not at all uncommon in Cairns, thanks to the crashing thunderstorms of the tropical north. That's the story

I'm going with when I arrive on the job a half a day late, but the truth is I missed my flight. I meander over to the airport bar, where a few pints will surely warm me up and give me courage for the mission on which I am about to embark. It takes less than an hour before I am shamelessly blurry-eyed, full of pizza and chocolate bars. In between masking my anxiety with booze and junk food and griping about layovers at the service desk, I worry and panic and recalculate how many beers I can drink before I am in danger of arriving not only five hours late but also perceptibly drunk. Probably one more, I always conclude.

Seven hours later, we cross the scorching hot tarmac and board a sixty or seventy seater plane to the isolated northern town of Weipa, Australia — population 1500. Everyone on board knows each other. Stricken with a sudden bout of shyness, I resort to eavesdropping on the conversation happening around me and feel comforted by what feels like authentic small-town gentility. A duty manager from the Albatross Bay Hotel picks me up from the airport. Even in the evening light the astounding beauty and lush greens of northern Queensland are everywhere in evidence. No one seems to mind my tardiness, since I won't be on the schedule for a day or two anyway.

The bugs are supersized. Even indoors there are grasshoppers the size of staplers and dozens of varieties of spiders. Days after I arrive, someone claims to have found a "huntsman" in the men's shower, the body of which is described as being big as a clenched fist, though it comforts me to know it's mostly the girls spreading such stories and that none of them have actually seen the offending arachnid. Still, a spider called a *huntsman* can't be good.

Less easily ignored is the toad population of Weipa, which is nothing short of biblical. Cane toads have been a major problem in Australia since their introduction in the thirties, when they made quick work of destroying the cane beetle and set about conquering the rest of the continent. They're big and ugly and *everywhere*. A feral species as heavy as four pounds, they have no natural predators in this country and are considered the number one threat to biodiversity in Australia.

With the heat, the bugs, the toads, and the snakes, no one spends much time outdoors except to smoke and drink at the pub. The staff quarters are as unpleasant as you might expect them to be but no worse. They are small and square like a cubicle, with enough room for a tiny closet, single bed, sink and bar fridge. You can cross the room in two strides, one and a half if you've got long legs. The air conditioners do their job adequately even if they leave a stale stink about the room and all over your clothes.

These makeshift apartments are for backpackers, after all, so the only solution is to make like a true traveller and not give a damn. They're attached together in blocks of eight, a structure that resembles a mobile home, or rather, a mobile apartment building with only one level. On the far end are two communal bathrooms, one for the ladies and one for the men, in a state of cleanliness not unlike a frat house, which is essentially what this is. I grin and bear it for three days before eventually knuckling down with a mop and bucket for a whole afternoon until it is restored to the point where I can at least use the shower without grimacing.

~

There are two principal occupations in Weipa and as such almost the entire town is employed either at the mines by Rio Tinto Alcan or at the detention centre by some facet of the Department of Immigration and Citizenship (DIAC). The rest of the population is employed in the service of DIAC and Rio Tinto's growing employee base, preparing their meals, stocking their shelves, and making their beds. Weipa is not a place many people choose to live in permanently, despite financial incentives from the government and the mines.

Employees of Rio Tinto occupy blocks and blocks of row houses all over the town, though I use the term "houses" loosely. Rio operates the largest bauxite mine in the country here in Weipa and also owns most of the town, either directly or indirectly. Properties have been built up on land leased from the aboriginals for boatloads of cash. Even the grocery store is subsidised by Rio Tinto, which nonetheless is said to be the most expensive in the country since all the goods have to be shipped in by barge or by plane. Though the town has no proper municipal government, it does have a town council, also funded by Rio Tinto.

Bauxite is everywhere; it is the very heart and soul of Weipa. It stains the dirt with the rich earthy red colour that is painted all over the town. It is in between your toes and in your hair and all over your clothes. Deep red termite mounds pop up everywhere, gothic insect castles decorating the red dirt roads. During the wet season you need a sturdy four-wheel drive just to get through the muck and down to the pub. In a town half populated by government employees, the streets are awash with white cars, every last one stained top to bottom in the exquisite red soil. When the rains do come, all roads out are closed and the only escape is by air or by sea.

Employees of DIAC and its co-contractors don't necessarily have it any better off than the miners. The lucky ones get to live at the hotel while the unlucky ones live in an old converted hospital. The hospital is dilapidated and messy. Most of the walls are no more than curtains. There are rumours of a cleaning staff, although hardly any attempt at even basic hygiene is in evidence.

It has one communal lounge room that is mostly used for the storage of empty beer cases ever since someone stole the TV. Every so often you hear of a new recruit demanding to be driven straight back to the airport.

The hotel is much better, for the most part. There are three grades of rooms: managerial staff, guests of the hotel, and miscellaneous workers (nurses, security officers, lawyers, etc.). The managers get the biggest, most modern units, the best of which might rival a three-star hotel. The second class of rooms is clean and renovated in a few key places, only smaller and slightly older. Lastly there are the dongas, a collection of duplex mobile homes on stilts, relegated to the back where no one can see them.

The Immigration employees work on a Royal Australian Air Force base at Scherger Immigration Detention Centre, about thirty kilometres outside of town. Employees sign a confidentiality agreement upon arrival, so the specifics of what everyone does there is all very hush-hush. The detainees are almost uniformly maritime refugees hoping to succeed in their claims for asylum in Australia. Though the Centre is said to be only temporary, enormous batches of detainees are flown in regularly. No one actually believes they will close. Down the road a new hotel is being built to house the growing population of workers.

~

The heat is so punishing that my brain is obstinately clouded and hazy. In the mornings on housekeeping duties I'm often ferried out to collect supplies for restocking the guest rooms. The blistering heat has got my memory in such a state that when I make a run to the supply cart I have to keep repeating, "towels, towels, towels," otherwise I forget what I came for. Even with the repetition, I only remember about half the time.

In the Belly of Oz

I can't get clean, even though I'm showering three times a day. I am perpetually covered in a sticky layer of grime that grows thicker by the hour. One morning during my first week it seemed impossible to escape the repugnant sticky-sweet odour in the motels. I doubled over in mortification when I realised that the smell was leeching out of my own filthy, sweating body. In between shifts, I'm tempted to lock myself in my refrigerated mobile cubicle and give myself over to the sanctity of cold showers and cool white sheets.

In the evenings I work in the hotel restaurant. It's a big place and all of the employees do double or triple-duty. As a waitress, I am a hopeless fraud. I spill drinks, break glasses and serve cab-sauv instead of sauv-blanc. My name appears over and over in the weekly waste report, which reads like my own personal journal of mispours, errors, and complaints. On my first night working at the restaurant, the owner abruptly removed me from bar duties and demoted me to plate collection. I am renowned for asking the most idiotic questions imaginable, for example, *"which plates should be served with steak knives?"* The young English bartender looks at me sourly and replies, *"umm, just the steaks dear."* As a barmaid, I am even worse. Thankfully, my exotic accent and sweet summer tan warrant more than a little bit of unjustified clemency for my ridiculous slip-ups and flagrant lack of any experience whatsoever in hospitality.

~

In mining country they say there are ten men for every woman. It's hard to verify this ratio exactly, but there's obviously something to it. The miners come down to the pub still dressed in their neon work shirts, dirt all over their faces — hardly the piano-playing creative types I'm used to back home. Still, I'm determined that Weipa is where I will find romantic redemption — in addition to all the joy, of course, but higher motives need not preclude more earthly ones. I'm a hot ticket item up here, even if that barely distinguishes me from any other women.

I am immediately comfortable and at home in Weipa and suddenly back to my old self again. Though I'm prone to do a lot of tough talking, the reality is that I'm still a big sucker for love. I can hardly go on one date without my mind jumping ten years down the track. As Jane Austen famously said, "A lady's imagination is very rapid." Mine is no exception. So when a handsome but discernibly intoxicated government worker makes moves on me during my Saturday night bar shift, I give him a coy smile and write him off. But back in my room at the end of the night, I keep thinking about him.

I'd seen him once before when I was lounging on the back deck outside the hotel bistro, which you have to cross to get from the guest rooms to the pub. His blond, curly hair and singlet make him look about as Australian as they come. And yet he has a loose, Canadian friendliness about him, and a ruggedness slightly softer than that of his compatriots. I could almost picture him in snow pants and ski jacket, cruising down a mountain on a snowboard somewhere in Whistler. So yes, I'd thought about him. Somewhat rapidly, even.

The next morning I see him again and though stricken with embarrassment since I am covered in my own syrupy filth and dressed in a hideous housekeeping uniform, I can't quite extract my eyes from his gaze. His hair is wet and slicked back; he must be going to work. He looks older now but more like a professional and actually winks at me as I go about my work. *Ugh.* Winking is the worst. Winking is what old men do to kids in the park. In spite of myself, this wink sets my heart beating wildly and I replay it in my head over and over for the rest of the day.

The following day I dress myself up properly and even put on make-up for the first time in weeks. It's too hot for such things this far north. Fancy clothes get stained in sweat and make-up only melts off in the heat. Tonight I'm working in the restaurant with its dim lighting and air-conditioning. Though I happen to know my fantasy-future-husband (like I said, rapid imagination) usually eats in the pub, it doesn't stop me from hoping. When he actually does walk in, I'm so hopelessly love-struck that I can't think of anything to say. The best I can do is to take his order with over-the-top enthusiasm. He orders the Crumbed Brie, somewhat awkwardly I might add, pronouncing it "bry," which, as an honorary French-Canadian and lifelong lover of cheese, makes me blush with embarrassment.

He introduces himself properly this time, Matthew, and I take it as a sign since back at the pub he had simply called himself Matt. This sober alter ego wants to be perceived as dignified and proper, a stand-up guy. From the simple use of his full given name, I infer that he is trying to impress me. Armed with what I imagine is concrete proof of his returning my affections, I start making inquiries about this mysterious Matthew (with whom by now I've already moved to an outback ranch in my fantasy life, where I ride horses, milk cows, and raise his children).

As in any small town, no business is private business. The Head of Housekeeping quips boldly, "he split with his misses so he's lonely now," as if she knew him personally. The housekeepers in general refer to him as "Mr. Handsome Man." His colleagues are equally generous in their narratives, though it takes time to place the person in question since no one in the real world actually calls him "Matthew." In any case, Mr. Handsome Man seems well liked and well respected up here.

Since he lives in one of the better rooms of the hotel, I determine that he is most likely a manager at Scherger, the detention centre. Finally I am able to recognise my privileged status as housekeeper. We are privy to a lot of private information. We know secrets about everyone. We know who's been sleeping in whose bed, what medications they take, if they read dirty magazines, and the degraded levels of hygiene they are willing to tolerate.

You can tell a lot from a person by what they've got in their hotel rooms. None of the housekeepers object when I request specifically that they leave room #29 for me — Mr. Handsome Man's room. If anything, they encourage me. I spend an hour cleaning it, though everyone knows a simple spray down and sheet change shouldn't take more than twenty minutes. I give his book collection a careful dust over (*Diary of a Jet Set Call Girl*, *Angelina Jolie: A Biography*, and *In My Own Words* by His Holiness the Dalai Lama) and conclude a woman's lingering influence. In the bathroom there is an unopened 4-pack of condoms, leading me to believe he might be expecting to get lucky, but not very. You don't go on a wild, post-breakup sexpedition with a 4-pack.

Mostly I just tidy the room with a bit of extra care, turning over greeting cards (there's one from a woman who shares his last name whom I surmise to be his mother), checking ID cards (he's 36), and making sure there are no anti-depressants, illegal drugs, or weird pornos (there aren't). He obviously lives on rice crackers and cans of tuna, though I've learned through a bit of careful observation that his diet is heavily subsidised with Jack Daniels and chicken schnitzel from the pub. Other than that I leave things pretty much as I found them, except for one infinitesimal clue, placing one ID card back on the counter face up even though I'm almost certain I found it face down.

Eventually I work up the courage to slip a note under his door, "*a certain waitress thinks you're pretty handsome, meet me for a drink at the pub — I get off at nine.*" When nothing comes of it I get all heartbroken again, drinking myself into a state with the miners and the aboriginals. But I stay the course like the soldier of love that I am (in fantasy land, we've already sold the ranch and moved back to Canada where the kids can start school and get to know their Canadian cousins).

Friday night my restaurant shift finishes early and I march back up to the pub to pursue no less than the level of romantic satisfaction that has eluded me for twenty-seven years now. No pressure. He's there, of course; Saturday is his only day off. My hands are visibly shaking by now since in his absence I've built him up to a place no man could possibly ever live up to. Also, I have another note in my pocket that I didn't have the guts to slip under his door earlier.

He introduces himself yet again, Matt, this time, and mentions something about taking Saturday off so we can drive up to Mapoon and see the wild brumbies. As if I wasn't already sold on this guy, now he wants to drive out to the bush and see the wild horses. Minutes into the first conversation we've had in our civilian attire, he puts his hand on my lower back and slides it down, saying something about my short skirt. It sounds sleazy on paper and in retrospect, it probably will be. In this moment though, I can't find the will to slap his hand away since it feels like something we have been doing for years, like it is exactly the way he is accustomed to greeting me.

We leave almost immediately, down to the dongas where he's got laundry that needs putting in the dryer. It's in the laundry room amid the humming of machines and the smell of soap powder that he chooses to tell me about his kids, teenage girls, and the dissolution of his seventeen-year marriage. He's unflinchingly honest, almost threatening in the reckless dissemination of information, perhaps trying to entice me to fold while I still have all my cards in hand. He puts the whole deck on the table and turns over each of his cards one by one, laying his heart bare. It's lover's poker; here's what I've got to play with, now will you check or will you bet? I'm reckless in matters of the heart, a courtship cowgirl, so obviously I charge ahead, guns blazing.

Over the next few days he makes himself available to me — doesn't hold anything back. Australians are generous by nature but this Australian generosity on steroids. His heart, his hands, and his mouth bleed generosity with the force of Niagara Falls. His pours words all over me and they are like a symphony because they are exactly the words I have been wanting to hear.

This is the feeling I have been wanting to feel. These are the looks I have been looking for and the sounds that I have been listening for. We make love with our eyes open, our hearts wrapped around each other like a glove. There's no denying his heart is still a bleeding, scratched up mess but he has chosen me to wrap the wounds in gauze and be his antiseptic. I am humbled by his goodness and by his inherent selflessness.

There is affection, there are words and most of all there is laughter. The sound of our laughter rings in the corridors from dawn until dusk, both literally and figuratively. We lie in bed for hours rehashing every word, every look and every touch leading up to this moment. We cannot stop our hands and our mouths from seeking each other. We grab on and we cannot let go.

Maybe what we are really trying to do is hang onto *this moment* forever. Matthew is more conscious of his battle scars than I am. His may be fewer but they run much deeper. I'm riddled with scrapes but they're just surface wounds.

Bit by bit I move my meagre possessions into his room, one or two at a time, thinking maybe if I do it slowly, the fates will take no notice and leave us in this perfect peace for a few more exquisite moments. He looks into me and craves to know me. He orders me to look him straight in the eyes and answer his questions over and over. I let myself learn him in a different way, searching the lines on his face and the texture of his laughter, trying to map out the highways of his heart.

Inexplicably, I feel no fear. The old familiar anxiety is no longer lurking behind the curtain of ecstasy. This Matthew is good people. Wherever this road goes, it will be the right place. Here we are at the end of the earth, in Weipa, the unlikeliest of places, and there is something strangely perfect about it. I'm pretty sure this is the universe taking care of us, saying, *"You've done well, you've been good and honest and true and for your efforts I will give this person to you."*

"Are you happy?" he keeps asking me, over and over. Yes, I'm so happy. I want this feeling to last forever.

Thirteen Days: A Love Letter

You gave me you and I gave you me on the eve of Christmas Eve. And I remember with perfect clarity the way you looked at me: the honesty, the sincerity and most of all the light in your perfect green eyes. Christmas Eve we laid in bed from morning until night. I studied you and you studied me. We laughed and laughed and then we laughed some more. I wrapped my legs around you and cradled your head in my hands and it felt like my first night on earth. Christmas Day when you went back to work I whiled away the hours in your room, eating fruitcake and willing each minute to pass by quicker.

There was a staff party that day, a Christmas celebration for all the homeless wanderers with no family and nowhere to go, of which there are many up north. Of course I had to go, even if I'd long since lost all interest. I pranced around dreamily, floating on a cloud, puffing nervously at the cigarettes I'd swiped from your room. I made a few pathetic attempts at conversation and chastised myself for not having more fun. I didn't drink much; I wanted to keep my wits about me. Christmas in a bar is depressing enough but without you the world had suddenly lost all meaning. So I snuck out early to the BBQ out by the dongas, where everyone was laughing and drinking wine and seemed to be having the time of their lives. Or maybe it's because you were there and so everything looked different. You kept kissing me and looking at me with that glint in your eyes, like the two of us shared a secret. We only stayed a few minutes after that.

Every day was our anniversary. At the end of each one you thanked me for another day and my heart gave off little pangs of malaise because it was overwhelmed and dumbfounded by what it was feeling. Your beautiful blond head lay on the pillow, you looked at me with raised eyebrows and said, "I like ya," the word "like" intoned an interval higher, as though the feeling was brand new and took you by surprise every time you felt it. You looked at me with love, your kind eyes dripping with affection and you spoke of your love for your children. You said you would like to have a child with me and though I was bowled right over by the intensity of your emotions, my instincts told me you were exactly correct in your unassuming desire to go forth and multiply with me, that this was most certainly our destiny. I clung to the moment and turned it around in my mind, examining it from every angle, looking for chinks along the fragile surface of our plans. I wasn't afraid even though you asked me over and over and challenged me to run away scared. Running would have been infinitely more difficult than staying.

I did your laundry and while I folded your clothes I gave thanks that the stars had aligned in such a way as to bring us to here and now. For a minute your dirty laundry, your crumpled towels, and damp sweaty socks were perfect bliss. Day Five, I called my mother and I told her you were "the one," an expression I used to make fun of other people for using. You said, "Thank you, Amy, for bringing me back to life," and I said, "Thank you, Matthew, for choosing me." I willingly and openly professed my love for you because I couldn't not say it for one more day, the current of emotion running in me like wild dogs ripe to burst out of their cages. The next day I found a scrap of fax paper and left a note on your table saying, "Please, will you to marry me?"

∼

No one will believe we are possible. They will scoff at the improbability of you and me and give us all kinds of wretched advice but who can blame them? Life has a habit of teaching us cynicism if we let it. Whole volumes of books have been written on the importance of facing up to the realities of the gritty real world. Life is not a story by Jane Austen, people will say. Too many women are looking for Rhett Butler when they should be settling down with a Charles Hamilton, chasing an Edward Cullen when they'd be better off with a Jacob Black. It's just not me though. I'm not the sort of person who goes in for all that reality stuff. I wanted the whole fairy tale. You, my dear, are the man for whom I'd been teaching myself not to hope.

So let's pay no heed to the cynics and resist the ugly magnetism of the stinking real world. As you and I have had the privilege to witness firsthand, love makes for the unlikeliest of outcomes. What use has it for such pragmatism? Now life is teaching us something different so let's try to pay attention. You and I, we exist. The proof is in the pudding. To me you are perfect. Why shouldn't you, of all people, get two loves? You've been a good man, a good husband and a good father. Show me a man that deserves this more than you. If you will do it all over again with me, I will do it with you. You can teach me all the things you learned the first time around and everything will be fresh again because, for me, all of this is new.

Forget the other loves and let your heart be still, my darling. I only want to love you. Rip out your bleeding heart and leave it in my care. I will hold it and caress it and wrap it in satin cloth, massage the ropes and cords bring them back to life. Then I'll stitch this heart to mine and give it back to you in a suitcase of solid gold. And when our suitcase gets too heavy to carry, as it does from time to time, we'll stand shoulder-to-shoulder, hoist it on our backs and forge a way ahead together.

New Year's Eve when you came home blind drunk, spilled your naked heart all over me and begged me to leave, I cried a little for myself because I was afraid you might have meant it, but mostly I cried for you because I couldn't stand to see you in such pain, to see you suffer so undeservedly. Your sweet heart, your loving heart, I felt sure from now on I would give and do anything to see you strong again, to see you standing tall like the man I know you are. You were writhing and thrashing and clutching the place where you were shot through the heart. I was sick with rum and worry and keeled over on the bathroom floor but even in your wretched state you stood behind me and held back my hair while I vomited up a year's worth of grizzly memories, both mine and yours. I felt the warmth and the love of your hands in my hair and I knew that we were okay and that the two of us could make it together. Afterwards I lay crumpled up in our bed while you slept on the other side of the room in protest. I rationalised for you and I felt fear for us, but mostly I knew that this was just part of the process and that everything would be all right.

And so I will give you everything if you will only brush your lips against my neck from time to time and stroke the small of my back with the tips of your fingers. And for each of our years together we will celebrate each other on the eve of Christmas Eve. We'll commemorate the occasion with looks and smiles and laughter and the company of each other.

~

Northern Australia has two seasons: rainy and dry. For rainy season in Weipa, it's unusually dry for weeks and weeks. Everyone is wondering where the rains are. It's almost January. The sky is grey and the thunder rumbles on for days but still the rains refuse to come. Nature is building the tension, warming up the crowd before the big performance. The skies continue their unearthly growling, building still more tension, like they're trying to orgasm but never quite making it there. The cloud cover is so thick we lose satellite service, devastating when you spend so much time indoors away from the gruelling heat. It's incredibly common up here but for anyone who is not local, it's very shocking to be suddenly without TV, phone or Internet service all because of a few clouds. We get restless. We feel like we need to move.

When the rains come, they come with a vengeance, like the seventh plague of Egypt. One morning it's sunny and blue and in the afternoon it's nothing but crashing thunder, lightning and rain, rain, rain. It will go on like this for days. The rains bring with them a sense of relief; when everything else is moving, it's okay to just be still. The tin roofs of Australia make a symphony of these rains. I keep my windows open and lay in bed listening to the rains fall for days.

Though the rains keep coming, the housekeeping doesn't stop. Mornings are still mostly sunny, and we try and finish cleaning the dongas as early as possible, before the rain starts. Still there are days when the rains come crashing down with no warning at 9:00 a.m. We run frantically back and forth to the laundry, covering the trollies in plastic bags and ourselves in great plastic raincoats. We almost always end up soaking wet, our feet so saturated in water you can hear the slosh, slosh as we make our way to shelter. Sometimes the rains are so biblical that all we can do is stand out on the covered balconies of the adjoining dongas, waving at each other through sheets of rain and laughing. Along with the rains come gales of biting wind worthy of a Canadian winter, powerful enough to blow us around and around the site as we fight our way back to the laundry, hanging onto our shirts and jackets.

Relief from the heat never seems to manifest no matter how much it rains, no matter how much the wind blows. Sometimes after it rains the temperature actually rises. There's a public pool in town, modern and well maintained. But it's at least a few kilometres away and in this heat that might as well be another country. Even more of a tease are the freshwaters creeks, cool and inviting, clear as glass and full of crocodiles. There are lakes you're supposed to be able to swim in, but no one will guarantee your safety.

Though everyone agrees there could be crocs anywhere, we plan a trip to Vyces (aka Killer Croc Creek) for an afternoon swim, against a lot of sound advice. A local that Matt knows from work has agreed to escort us. Shaq is an aboriginal so he knows things about crocodiles, where they are likely to be at what time of year. More importantly, he's got a shotgun in his trunk and he knows how to use it. A group of us are still humming and hawing and dipping our toes in the water when Shaq jumps in, explaining that crocs always swim toward the ocean. Since there are some other swimmers a few hundred feet up the creek, we should be all right. Comfort indeed.

But it's worth it. The water is cleaner and fresher than anything I've ever seen. It's cold, clear and perfect; the ultimate antidote to a Weipan summer. Shaq barbeques a dozen varieties of meat in the back of the truck while his wife goes on croc-watch. I float on my back for hours watching the frigates overhead fighting against the wind and realising for the first time that today of all days the rains have held off for a whole afternoon. Life seems full of little miracles.

On Saturday afternoons when it does rain — every single other one — we lay in bed all day watching a variety of sports and playing the occasional game of gin-rummy. Since we don't get American channels out here what we are actually doing is watching live updates of the NBA scoreboard on the Internet. At first it feels strange, even sort of pathetic, but after a few weeks of small-town living it comes to feel completely normal. The last few minutes of the game are often made even more suspenseful by frequent power outages and unreliable Internet service. At some point the nearest and only cell tower is hit by lightning and we're out of service for two weeks.

I'm not really a sport-watching type of woman but that's what love and Weipa have made of me. Sometimes I even bet on the horses. On the other side of the world, you get really courageous. You can be and do anything. You're free to invent yourself from scratch. Really though, I don't want to become someone new. I'm ready to be who I am now. If that means letting go of the person I was, I'm ready to do it. I feel strong now. Strong enough to start cleaning skeletons from my closet, maybe shed the skin of the person I thought I wanted to be. The other person I invented but never quite became.

The Whole Truth

I am no stranger to love. Falling in love is central to my character. It is one of the fundamental qualities that define Amy — someone who falls in love easily (too easily, some will say), someone who is always dreaming, always pining for someone she met in a café or a train station, someone who is always getting her heart broken. That's Amy: Love Junkie. This Matthew may be special but he is by no means an anomaly.

Observe. I have been jilted by three men since coming to Australia, where I fled shortly after being unexpectedly dumped by the last "love of my life," who deserves at least some credit for my high-tailing the hell out of Montreal in the first place.

Such a staggeringly high number in such a small amount of time, it behooves me to pose the question: is it me? Is there some glaringly obvious dating faux pas I am repeatedly committing or perhaps a manual I've neglected to read? Could all these men have coincidentally missed all of the glorious and charming personality traits I am famous for? Or maybe, just maybe, is it just possible that my fondness for toothpicks and obsession with King Henry VIII are not as glorious and charming as I have come to believe? In the spirit of new beginnings, I'm making a no-holds-barred examination of my romantic failures this year; shed the snakeskin of regrets in which I have been slithering around, mop up the congealed carnage of my four-times-troubled heart and leave it for the ocean to wash away.

~

The first man to have had the pleasure of breaking my heart will be referred to as "Jean-Marc." Jean-Marc was generous and good-natured, a good old-fashioned French-Canadian mama's boy. He would do anything for me, if only he could recall what it was I had asked. He loved to smoke pot and was high for most of our three-year affair. He had a white board in his kitchen to aid his cannabis soaked brain, if only he could remember what it was he was trying to remember. Much like my sister and I, he loved him some lollies and could eat them by the bagful, wash them down with a beer or green tea, and follow them up with a variety of chocolate bars or a whole pack of *Gauloises* for dessert. He was a classic stoner.

Not surprisingly, my foremost memories of Jean-Marc are of lounging on the sofa in the evening-time, watching episode after episode of *Battlestar Galactica* in the cat hair forest that was his living room futon. His parents had a house in the country and so once in a while we would drive to a different city, sit on a different couch and watch different episodes of a different series. In the course of our relationship, we watched seven seasons of *24* (in the spirit of full disclosure, that's 168 hours of Jack Bauer). Our sex life was not exactly Casanovian — there was just too much good television that needed watching. But I loved Jean-Marc so desperately I could hardly hold it against him.

In our first year, the love that I felt for Jean-Marc was powerful enough to keep me from sleep. I would find myself sitting bolt upright at 3:00 a.m., seized by the sheer panic of blinding, epic, three-volume-novel love. By the second year, I relaxed into that love enough to address some more mundane worries. Jean-Marc loved me well enough but not in the gone-off-the-rails, lay-down-on-train-tracks-for-you way that I loved him. Despite the fact that I was just 135 pounds, did yoga daily and was in nearly the best shape of my life, he never quite let me forget that, physically speaking, I was not really his type. But I was happy and in love so I forgave him the mediocrity of his emotions as well as his penchant for starving supermodels, even resisting the temptation to conform to his notion of the feminine ideal — for a time, anyway.

Jean-Marc's family became my family. His mother became my mother. We celebrated holidays, attended baptisms, and took family photos. Despite knowing that Jean-Marc had some major doubts, I began planning our future. Meanwhile, Jean-Marc was painfully careful about his use of the word "we" when we got to discussing the great milestones of our lives. He remained coolly detached; driving home from dinner on a Saturday night, he would casually float the idea of his moving to Japan for a year. Nevertheless, I persisted in making excuses and giving explanations, meticulously crafting the theory that Jean-Marc would eventually come around. Some part of me must have known that to address these concerns would no doubt lead to the inevitable demise of our romantic association.

Sure enough, three and a half years later, long after the sad death of Jack Bauer's first wife Teri but just before the destruction of the Cylon resurrection ship, Jean-Marc got cold feet. Like many men before him, Jean-Marc was forced to come clean about his long-term projections for our relationship when the subject of cohabitation was finally raised. If I hadn't been choking in the death grip of law school and suffering from an academically and romantically induced eating disorder, I might have been able to forgive him his callous and poorly timed dismissal of my affections. But forgiveness, as I have learned, is a noun and not a verb. God knows I made some mistakes myself.

~

The second man to chuck me this year was César, my Latino Ken Doll. I'm still sorting out what happened there. One minute I was casually seducing a former piano student, cool as a cucumber, prematurely proclaiming myself finally free from the emotional cul-de-sac that was Jean-Marc aka the former-future-father-of-my-children. Next thing I knew I was shamefully crying my eyes out on a 75 cent per minute international phone call while César coolly informed me he would like me to "be free and have fun," whatever that meant.

I'd begun seeing César just a month or so after Jean-Marc left, although "seeing" is a bit of a stretch since the acts we performed together in no way resembled a romantic connection. Though it didn't seem that either of us found much romantic satisfaction in our encounters, we dragged out for five long months. We met for drinks and dinner every second week at the most, although there were month-long stretches where we wouldn't see each other at all. While I had always thought of César as handsome, an emotional attachment refused to materialise no matter how hard I pushed. Toward the end of the summer I grew to almost dread our sporadic "dates" and would work myself into a state days leading up to the big day.

Then one day César magically won me over with something so mundane, he probably never even noticed it happening. To be fair, I was trying hard to like him — he was musical and handsome, had a good job with a steady income and was looking to buy a home. He was your classic "good on paper" guy. It was several months into our affair. We'd been to the driving range and then out to dinner. Over a plate of meat piled about a foot high that César had taken the liberty of ordering for us (which, as a former vegetarian, I found not only excessive but just a little grotesque), I finally let on to César that I just wasn't feeling it.

He nodded along seeming to understand and yet for some reason, after he'd picked up the cheque and we'd left the restaurant, kept leaning in to kiss me passionately. On the way home he started talking about the novel he had written and how he had recently begun working on another. He apparently loved books as well. We did the book lover's dance, raved about our favourites and indulged each other by listening while the other raves about his own. It thrilled me, put me in the mood for love. In my defence, it can feel like a real connection; if you love the thing you're talking about enough, it's easy to confuse the love of that thing for love of the person in front of you. But I then I confuse a lot of things with love, as I would later learn.

The real clincher was when I mentioned *The Singularity* and began rhapsodizing about my attachment to Ray Kurzweil. César had also heard of *The Singularity* and showed a benign interest in it himself. In retrospect, I'm not even sure he'd read it. I was so excited to be talking books and he seemed sort of familiar with the subject. And that's it. I am ashamed to say that's all it took — someone who claimed to have written a novel and was mildly interested in scientific truth. I wasn't too picky back then.

I say that he *claimed* to have written a novel because, no matter how hard I pushed, he would never actually show it to me. And one fateful evening I caught a popular Argentinian film with a strikingly similar plot to the one he'd laid out for his novel. I got a shock in my chest and instantly some part of me just *knew*. I couldn't actually call his bluff because I wasn't entirely sure of it myself. But it was always there in the back on my mind. I couldn't erase the knowledge.

In spite of my doubts, I could no longer avoid the obvious fact that César was not always 100% truthful on a number of accounts. For one thing, he would never bring me back to his house, nor would he stay the night at my apartment. He claimed to have taken in his parents who had recently emigrated from Mexico, which was probably true. Although sometimes I would ask him what he'd done that day and there would be a telltale pause before he explained that he'd spent the morning shopping with his mother. There was something suspect about his mannerisms. I'd given him piano lessons for two years before it came out he had a five-year-old daughter. Another six months later it came out that he'd been married to the mother of this child. By then I was afraid to ask if he was actually divorced. Even the alleged ex-girlfriend that he had coincidentally broken up with right as I was breaking up with Jean-Marc had a curiously fake-sounding name: Shelly.

He never offered to drive me to the airport but then he was careful about establishing precedent. When I suggested we exchange letters by post to keep the romance alive, he refused to give me his address, saying he'd be moving in a couple of weeks. Though as the weeks flew by, this mysterious future house never seemed to come to fruition. After I'd crossed the ocean, contact grew less and less frequent, until he hardly bothered with the minutest of greetings more than once or twice per week.

I was devastated by his sudden lack of interest. My heart was only just beginning to seal its wounds when César made quiet work of splitting them open again. I rebounded quickly though, perhaps because my emotions for him were mostly founded on pure imagination. A few weeks after the infamous instruction to "be free and have fun," César informed me it was in fact a test — a test that I had promptly failed without even knowing I was being examined. But by then I didn't care since I was already hopelessly in love with Klaus, the German backpacker who rolled through town for 36 blissful hours and tortured my heart for at least as many miserable days. Fickleness, thy name is woman.

~

Klaus was so crushingly beautiful I had to wear my eyeglasses in bed, his skin perfectly smoothed by tropical beaches and blond hair impeccably coloured by the Australian sun. Just twenty-five years old, poor Klaus had no idea how to make love. He was clumsy and selfish; he would roll off and fall asleep immediately after. With his soft skin and infectious smile, I guessed he would probably never have to learn. He taught me to love campervans, to prepare a kangaroo steak and to laugh until my heart bubbled to the point of explosion. After Klaus, the peace I had unwittingly found in Hervey Bay and subsequently taken for granted was suddenly gone, never to be heard from again.

I had met Klaus in a bar on the esplanade, just a few blocks from our house. His Argentine companion had introduced him to my sister, in hopes they might hit it off. The fact that I went chasing after this young man, who frankly demonstrated significantly more interest in my sister, speaks volumes about my confidence at the time. Once her marital status became known and she'd established herself as a loyal wife, I was the natural alternative. Klaus had also been recently dumped, by his girlfriend of several years. Though he was clearly distraught and still in love with her, he masked his pain by dancing wildly and drinking liberal amounts of cheap, Australian swill.

He kissed me in his dreadful European way, like he was uncorking a bottle of cheap wine with his tongue. I had experienced this before, first in a wily Frenchman on the streets of Paris in my early twenties and later in César. Perhaps there are

European women who enjoy this but I believe it's the mark of a man that has never loved before. In any case, I don't mind admitting I'm old fashioned when it comes to kissing; I like a bit of tenderness. Uncorking tongue be damned, I still stayed in his camper van for two idyllic nights before he hit the road, swearing he would return again and soon.

We promised to meet in Noosa the following week when I would join his travelling band of ruffians at the caravan park where they were staying. Just as I was confirming bus times and packing my suitcase for the third time, Klaus sent me a message explaining in broken English that he'd met with "two guys" who were keen to hitch a ride all the way to Sydney, which would mean big savings in fuel and campsite fees. I was inconsolable. In a new all-time low, I'd been dumped for gas money. I later discovered on Facebook that "two guys" was in fact a young Swedish woman, blond and tanned and living the backpacker life I was aching to live myself.

~

My final foray into the world of heartache was a way to bide my time while I made other plans. I felt certain this would be my chance to be the heartbreaker instead of the heart being broken. Not that I looked forward to it but I did relish the idea of regaining some of my dignity and desirability as a partner. But I was lonely and so I let it drag out. Before I knew it, Number Four had beaten me to the punch again.

Number Four was Mark, the car rental shop guy who nicked my information from the insurance waiver, which I thought was cute but anyone else would have called creepy. It was the first time an Australian man had paid any attention to me and though I would hardly have described him as handsome, I was lonely and relished any attention I could get. Just weeks later, in a sudden turn of events, he went from texting me eight times a day to flatly ignoring weekend invitations to keep me company. When he could no longer disregard me without looking like a jerk, he explained in a text message that he'd made the decision to give it a second go with his ex-girlfriend. Though my heart was far from broken, it poked at an open wound hardly just beginning to congeal.

~

So there it is: the whole truth. It's obvious the prevailing theme is wilful blindness. I learned it with Jean-Marc, perfected it with César, and then plied my trade with Klaus and Number Four. Probably it says something deep and damaging about my character — I failed to face up to the evidence staring me in the face — but I prefer to look at it as evidence of incurable romanticism.

Sure I played it fast and loose with my heart but at least I put my cards on the table. A cynical person will write me off as the world's biggest tramp and observe that I myself invited the heartache by casting my nets into the ocean so frivolously. A romantic person will know that the human heart is wild and can hardly be expected to respond to something so arbitrary as reason and logic. Bah! What use have I for realism? Would a realist skip the continent and the promise of a lucrative legal career just to get her heart broken by a twenty-five-year-old kite-surfer?

Maybe the heart is just a little more fragile in the southern hemisphere. Maybe it's all the sharks. Maybe it's me. This is probably the part where I say something about how no romantic relationship can compare to the one you have with yourself. As Oscar Wilde says, *"to love oneself is the beginning of a lifelong romance."* That's the relationship that matters most. However shabbily any of those men treated me, I've done much worse to myself in the last twelve months. The truth is, I still have a thing or two to learn about self-love, about treating myself with dignity and respect. I suppose that's part of why I came to Australia — to give myself a second chance.

Knotty Valentine

There is an invisible cord running along the corridors of the distances between us. It is knotted around our perfect atriums and looped through the delicate ventricles of our beating red hearts, one end secured to mine and the other secured to yours. When you are away, it is this cord that connects me to you. And when you are nearby, in the next room or down the hall or checking on the cricket scores, there is this all-consuming urge to seize hold of that cord with both hands and reel you in to me. But it's when your head is heavy or your heart is weary that our cord is pulling the hardest, tugging at me with the force of an ocean, a gentle tidal wave pulling me back to your shores. It's the love that binds me to you.

May the length of our rope grow in proportion to the love we give to each other. May we give each other the spaces and the room to grow, to trip on our rope without loss of love, to tie it in knots and tie it in bows. And may we love those spaces in the same way we love the absence of space between us. May the fibre of our rope be sturdy as the substances from which we are made, tough as our teeth and thick as our blood. In storms may it bind us and be the wind in our sails, may it stand under pressure of hammers and nails.

When it snaps in half, we'll tie ourselves back together using all the knots we know, starting with the "Simple Sailor's Please Don't Break My Heart Knot," and later the "Figure Eight Forgiveness Knot," the "French Bowline Believe in Me Knot," the "Lighthouse Watchman's Where Were You Last Night Knot," the "Half Hitch Home from the Hospital Knot," and of course the "Inline Looping I Take Back What I Said Knot." When we don't know the knot we'll invent one together and if it comes apart we'll try another. As our rope grows smaller it will gather us together until the day that we tie our very last knot, the "Two Strand Overhand This Isn't Goodbye it's Only the Beginning Knot." This last knot will seal our hearts together forever and send one of us off into the great abyss until later we'll join again one with the other, forge a new rope and a new forever.

Sweet Dreams, Darling

Sometimes it is you that is making the waves and sometimes it is the waves that are making you. Some days you are navigating the surly waters with a seemingly natural ease and moments later it is the seas that are knocking you back in your place, compelling you once again to put forth some dreary questions about destiny, circumstance, free-will, and the way the cookie crumbles.

This very evening I am lying in Matt's hotel bed, the frigid, artificial temperature a perfect juxtaposition to the sticky yet similarly unnatural heat of a Weipan summer, curling my toes under a thick blanket the way I used to, back home in the deep of a cold, Canadian winter. The irony of this is lost on me, as I lose myself in the cavernous green eyes of my lover and the manner in which we have tangled ourselves to form a human pretzel, leaving the exposed parts of our writhing bodies to fend for themselves. Moments later I am navigating the shadowy dirt roads of this remote country town, racing through the impossibly provincial darkness to the hospital. Matthew is moaning audibly in the passenger seat, cradling his head in his hands while my own head is barrelling back and forth between *ANEURYSM! ANEURYSM! ANEURYSM!* and *GOOD GOD WOMAN, GET IT TOGETHER!*

The doctor looks him up and down with an insufferably straight face and says, *"Now don't be alarmed sir but I think your brain may be haemorrhaging and even though it is possibly nothing we are calling in the Royal Flying Doctor Service to take you into the city this very second for further testing maybe just a CT scan and perhaps a spinal tap but again it might be nothing."* Relaxed though the doctor is, I can't help noting that she has reminded me to remain calm at least three times in under 60 seconds.

There's nothing subtle about a spinal tap. Half-heartedly I attempt to imitate the doctor's relaxed demeanour, massaging Matthew's aching temples and nodding along as I digest this unnerving turn of phrase, arranging my face in a way I hope looks composed yet concerned, it probably looks like I'm suffering from a bad stomach ache.

The nurse hands me the paperwork as though I am logically the best person for the job, which flatters me, making me feel so undeservedly special that I can't quite admit that my factual knowledge of Matthew is alarmingly scant. With hesitation I fill in his first and last name (is it one *t* or two?) then discreetly root through his wallet to check the spelling and fill in the missing information, which is nearly everything else. Under primary contact I write my own name even though, legally speaking, I am in fact at the bottom of the proverbial food chain and have no claim whatsoever to such a privileged position on the patient's contact sheet. Under power of attorney I grimace and write down his mother's name, tapping away at his mobile phone for her information even though it doesn't take a law student to know for certain that, barring other arrangements of which I am evidently unaware, power of attorney automatically falls to my lover's estranged wife. But it's far too late at night and I'm already far too flustered to open that Pandora's Box.

While Matt awaits the Flying Doctors, I'm commissioned to make a run back to the hotel and collect a few personal effects for the journey. The plane is patients-only so I'll have to make my own travel arrangements in the morning; it's only a few hours away anyway. Back in Matt's company car I endeavour to compose myself and summon my inner driving teacher; start engine, lights on, hand brake off, check blind spot, reverse: things that should have been second nature by now if only I hadn't lived in the city for so many years and never properly learned to drive. Once again navigating the country dirt roads in the inky black night, I train my brain onto a quick check list just to hold it steady; toothbrush, underwear, cell phone, clean clothes, toiletries. When I can't find any cell phones in under 20 seconds, I spin into a panic, frazzled to such a degree that by the time I get back in the car to return to the hospital, I drive a half kilometre with the lights off.

The paramedics fetch Matt from the ER and the two of us exchange an absent-minded goodbye at which I am only half present since most of my energy is already engaged in a vicious sort of divine bargaining of his behalf, laced with loose threats of spiritual revolt. Back at the Alby I manage one heroic hour of sleep before rising to exchange car keys, provide explanations and strategize with my lover's colleagues, at which point enormous, raindrop-size tears start spilling all over my face with hardly any warning. This process is repeated later on in the morning with each of my three bosses; head of housekeeping, the night-time duty manager in charge of the rosters, and eventually the hotel manager.

By late afternoon I am on a plane and by evening I am back in my lover's arms. By this time, he has been through a battery of tests confirming bleeding in his brain, the cause of which the doctors have given a host of hypotheses but no clear explanation, and checked him out of the hospital with a few nicotine patches and orders to take a low daily dose of aspirin. This kind of ambivalent, slapdash doctoring is now the global standard, in Australia as it is in Canada.

While it's not exactly the lovers' getaway I've imagined, his employer puts him in a hotel and the doctors neglect to provide a fit-to-fly certificate and recommend a few days convalescence, providing us with a couple of days together during which we assume the pretzel once again, eat pizza in bed, watch *Words and Numbers* and imagine ourselves on a real vacation rather than a medically enforced sabbatical. Every hour is savory sweet as apple pie, iced with a delectable garnish of *possibility*, of another hour, another day, and another year together. We're alive after all; better to make the most of it. For two days we frolic together in the hotel pool for hours, sun ourselves on the deck, and sip $15 cocktails from the swim-up bar. In this way the whole jarring ordeal becomes an occasion for our love to blossom and grow, a chance to say things we couldn't say before, to let go the worries of yesterday and bask in the encircling warmth of each other.

Later I'm sure we'll laugh about the expression "Flying Doctors" and maybe add it to a growing list of endearing Australian cultural nuggets but hereafter, every night while Matt sleeps I secretly roll over and gaze at him with just the teensiest bit of hysteria, anxious to locate the subtle rise and fall of his chest, to reassure myself that he is at least alive.

For a while Matthew is shocked by his own mortality and proposes sweeping life changes to ensure his health and longevity. The majority of these changes fall flat when, a few weeks later, he forgets his mortality even swifter than the speed at which he was reminded of it, only this time his actions have got a glossy new coat of denial. I bitch and nag and throw my arms in the air for some time afterward but eventually I give it up, let him do what he wants with his body.

Eventually life will go on as it always does and sooner or later the shock of it all will wear off. From time to time we'll take one another for granted again, forgetting the hard lesson we learned until one day something extraordinary jerks us back into remembering the precious gift we've been given and teach us gratitude once more.

~

Matthew's father and grandfather both died of a heart attack. Matthew's dad had only just hit sixty when he died and his mother is still holding it against his dad. He had quit smoking three months before he died. Naturally she blamed him for not doing it sooner. Quitting, I mean. The way she saw it he'd chosen cigarettes over her, which is sort of true if you think about it. Isn't it a given nowadays that if you smoke you're going to die young? We don't hear nearly as many stories anymore about grandparents and aunts and uncles who live to ninety-five and smoked until the day they died. Those days are gone, maybe because there are so many additional carcinogens now in our day-to-day life. You're lucky enough to survive cosmetics, KFC and foam packaging, without the additional health risk of a pack a day.

You can't choose how you go but there are a number of dramatic ends you can almost rule out by making a few smart choices. We all do our best with what we have, try to make choices that will keep us alive the longest. That's the easy part, really. The real trick is to let others make their own choices, decide for themselves how much risk they are willing to take. You can't choose which of your teenagers are going to sneak out to rave parties on the weekend and how many cigarettes a day your partner is going to smoke. It's hard enough to discourage your friends from drinking and driving. Nobody likes to be told what to do. The more you tell someone not to do something, the more disappointed you are when he eventually does it.

I grew up in a nice, Christian family. There were some strange things going on in our house but no more than in anyone else's house. My childhood was as unusual as the next. We had some exceptional rules but we grew up in a comfortable home. We lived on a quiet street in a small town. Our parents loved us and spent a great deal of time teaching us the difference between right and wrong. We read the bible for an hour every day after sitting down to a home-cooked meal. Our lawn was always mowed and my mother planted flowers every year before anyone else on the block. You always knew spring was coming because there'd be tulips coming up in front of the house.

None of that stopped me from smoking crystal meth in the girl's bathroom during science class when I was fourteen, or any of the other picket-fence neighbourhood kids from buying up sheets of acid and selling hits out in the smoke pit of the local high school.. You just don't get to choose what kind of reckless activities your loved ones will choose to engage in. The more expectations you put on them, the more disappointed you'll get when they don't make the choice you thought was the right one. I learned that from Jean-Marc. Jean-Marc smoked joints from the time he woke up to the time he went to bed. He worked fewer hours than I did, even when I was a full-time student. He lived in an apartment that his parents owned and drove a car that they had also purchased for him. Though I don't have the evidence to prove it, I suspect they also gave him an allowance.

Jean-Marc had a free ride. But I wanted him to be chasing success as hard as I was. I wanted him to be able to support a family or at least keep the goddamn house clean. Since I'd written him into my future as the father of my children and lifelong caretaker of my heart, I saw it as his duty to pursue a career, give up his filthy habits, or at least vacuum the damn rug once in a while. Looking back, Jean-Marc had it made. He had all the time in the world to play in rock bands, get high, and fiddle around on his laptop. People would kill for that opportunity. Isn't that why people buy lottery tickets? You think it's so they can take extravagant vacations and live in ten-bedroom houses but really it's because we all secretly crave to lay on the couch all day and work when we feel like it, without the pressure of paying phone bills and mowing the lawn.

At the time, I was convinced he'd be happier if he went off into the world and *accomplished* things. It frustrated me to no end that he never seemed able to finish anything. Who was I to have such opinions? Of all people, I was hardly one to advise him. It's not as if the pursuit of success was working so well for me. I was just as miserable as he was. The difference is that I was carrying the additional weight of a partner who was constantly letting me down. It got to a point where I suddenly couldn't even stand the smell of his cigarettes. Not just in a non-smoker kind of way, but in a full on, stick-you-head-out-the-window-and-vomit way. It's strange how you can love someone so dearly and loathe him so deeply at the same time. But then maybe it wasn't even love; maybe it was something else.

Whatever it was, being with Jean-Marc taught me to manage my expectations. It taught me to be careful about putting pressure on other people to aspire to what I thought was their destiny. What do I know about destiny? Mine seems to change with the seasons. Trying to live up to others' expectations is what landed me in law school. I don't want to do that to others any more than I want them to do it to me. It's not about being hard as rock and doing everything on your own; it's about finding your own happiness independent of the actions of those around you. When it comes down to it, if Matthew isn't keen to take care of his health, it's not for me to criticise. He's a grown man; he can choose for himself if he wants to stay up past ten o'clock. I'm determined not to repeat the mistakes I made with Jean-Marc. It's not fair to anyone, least of all me.

The Washbasin(s) of Australia

The housekeepers are a rare and delightful breed. It doesn't take long before I fall in love with them too. They're tough yet jovial, feminine yet foul-mouthed, gossips in the laundry room yet discreet amongst the guests. They're my kind of people — I feel infinitely more comfortable among the housekeeping staff than I do among the waitresses and barmaids with whom I am far closer in age.

Darlene, for example, takes pride in the way she makes the washbasins sparkle. Occasionally I too take some measure of pride at having blossomed into a semi-credible waitress. My aptitudes in the serving industry have progressed to the point where I can call myself a waitress without feeling like a desperate fraud. Meanwhile I can say with absolute authority that I take no such pride in making anyone's washbasins sparkle. Still, mopping black grime off the kitchen floors and unearthing the clay coloured tiles buried underneath all the scum is not exactly dignifying but it is in some way oddly gratifying, so maybe we are not so different after all, Darlene and I.

Between the four of them, the housekeepers have put in several decades of service at Albatross Bay Resort. The latest addition, Suchin, is newly emigrated from Thailand and artfully dedicated to avoiding doing any actual work. She speaks English only selectively, meaning when it suits her to understand, she does and when it doesn't, she doesn't. When you try speaking to her, she responds with a vacant, bemused gaze and goes about her business. The rest of us proceed relatively unruffled by her pretensions to vacuity and go about our own business. Suchin is by no means a beauty nor does she appear to possess any exceptional cleverness. Her skills in English comprehension are still undetermined. Her expression is one of perpetual uncertainty.

And no wonder. What a cruel joke to secure an Australian husband only to find yourself pulling ten hour days as a cleaning lady in this lonely outback town. Some days I find her standing idly in an empty motel room, staring into space. It'll be a room she cleaned that very morning so you might think she has returned to replace the shampoo bottles or deliver fresh towels but you can never be quite sure. Other days it will take her forty-five minutes to stock the trolley and bring around fresh cleaning supplies, a job any one of us might have completed in five minutes. Is she taking a break she badly needs, a necessity she is unable to verbalise? Perhaps she is simply lazy. If the former, I commend her. If the latter, then I prefer to think of her as overtired and overworked. Her husband works in the mines so they mustn't lack for money. And yet whatever they have never seems to be enough. When her hours get cut, this charming man rings up and barks at Marta, our head of housekeeping, in a furious rage. I hope he does not speak to Suchin in this manner.

Darlene is a different sort of enigma. She'll talk you under the table any day of the week, with minimal regard to the amount of energy put into actually listening. You'd think this would make her an unpleasant sort of person but really it is her most endearing quality. Her voice has an appealing lull to it, her stories repeated often enough that you can listen with half an ear, knowing if you miss a few details, you'll pick them up on the next run. Every now and again you'll be expected to provide commentary, but nearly all of the time a simple *"mmm-hmm"* or *"oh, man!"* is more than adequate. She has an obvious maternal nature and yet her speech is peppered with curse words, even on days when she brings her eleven-year-old granddaughter, Jenny, to work. *"This is fuckin' bullshit,"* she'll say, when one of the rooms is particularly dirty, *"I reckon we should be paid more." "Whada you think?"* Darlene's questions are almost always loosely rhetorical.

I happen to know that Darlene's mother was a kind of gypsy and that Darlene travelled Australia by caravan for most of her formative years. She talks about her youth like it was a grand adventure and I do believe it was. I also know that she laboured for years, maybe decades, as a fruit picker. She was in the fields picking potatoes six months after giving birth to her first child. Darlene had two children before she was even nineteen, and lost her first husband in an accident when she was still in her early twenties. For all that, she keeps it light in conversation and it seems like her heart is comparably unscarred, or at least finely polished with the balm of time. She doesn't *need* the work and yet somehow, unfathomably, she *likes* housekeeping, although that probably says more about the town than it does about the housekeeper. Darlene has learned to appreciate simple pleasures, notably the easy joy of having done a hard day's work.

My favourite of Darlene's recounts is the story of her younger sister. This one came up for the second time when Darlene was delivering her thoughts on Demi Moore's romantic connection, post-Kutcher era, with Zack Efron, who is more than twenty years her junior.

"My sister, y'now, she's forty now, left her husband for a 22-year-old. They had this big, flash wedding, ten thousand dollars, moved into an enormous beach house, beauooo-tiful polished floors like, bi-i-i-g 57-inch flat screen TV, had a real good life. She left him like, said he was 'boring.'"

That's how Darlene talks — clipped phrases punctuated with audible italics.

"He bought her a cleaning business, sixty thousand, she done real well, built it up real big like. I seen her give that young bloke five hundred dollars, said 'here, go shoppin'.' He come back an hour later and ask for more! 'Whadja buy,' she said, 'coupla boardies, few shirts, y'know. His mother died like so she took the sister in, got chest pains middle of the day, the guy that come 'round was real rude to her, so she said 'I got no use for you,' sent him away, died that night in her sleep, heart attack. That family they took allota drugs like …"

The story goes on for a mile and still my understanding of it is a bit shaky, even after the second run. Darlene hardly ever uses names so it's difficult to follow all the characters. You never really get the whole gist of it until you've heard it a few times. Her stories range from the enthralling to the mundane and are mostly full of gaps and failing to abide by a clear timeline. She tells stories inside of other stories that are themselves laced with invisible parentheses. She won't be inconvenienced with climaxes, punch lines, or even the necessity of a central character. Still her tangential narratives provide an agreeable soundtrack to what is otherwise a relatively bland career in toilet cleaning. And besides, it's nice being able to tune in and out as I like, kind of like AM radio.

At break time we all go back to the laundry and sit around the picnic table for about forty-five minutes. In Australia this is called "smoko" or "morning tea." Smoko is supposed to last fifteen minutes but we all pretend we're not looking at the clock. We drink tea and eat chocolate from the bar fridge, supplied by the guests of the Alby who are always leaving boxes of chocolate as tokens of appreciation. Sometimes we sit in silence reading gossip magazines but more often we sit listening to Darlene spin her stories.

Marta, head of housekeeping, usually sits down with us for smoko, even though she works in the laundry and isn't on the same schedule. She's got a calendar on the fridge that she uses to cross off the days one box on at a time, like she's counting down to a birthday. Except she's not counting down to anything, it's just something she does. One time Marta worked every single day for three months without a day off. She used to come around the pub sometimes on her days off, but she hardly has days off anymore. Anyway, as Marta says, "These days it's nothing but cocks and balls down there." I have no idea what that means but I love when Marta says things like that. At smoko she sits down with a pack of cigarettes and a miniature can of Heinz beans or spaghetti, which she eats lukewarm, straight from the can.

Guests are always stopping by for a chat at smoko, since you have to pass the laundry to get to the parking lot. They tell us all kinds of things in secret. We're like lawyers or psychotherapists; there is an implied confidentiality. We get all the information before anyone else. We're the first to know if someone's been fired, who's been cheating on his wife, or when the next top-secret transfer of detainees is being conducted at Scherger. We keep it in the vault, to be sure, but that doesn't stop us from gossiping aggressively amongst ourselves.

On Wednesdays, when it's just Darlene and me, smoko takes on a whole new meaning. In addition to a forty-five minute "morning tea," we have a number of quiet sit-downs in the garden, a forty-five minute lunch and, at the end of the day, a final sit-down in the laundry. For our final smoko we go down to the bottle shop and use our tips to buy beers. Back at the laundry, we pour our beers into coffee mugs and sit around sipping for another forty-five minutes before heading back up to the office and signing out.

Lorraine, a part-time housekeeper, is an inspiration to us all. Just the other day at smoko, she declared that she and her husband plan to save $40,000 this year. Why? Because they can, I assume. Lorraine's husband works in the mines, as do the husbands of all four housekeepers at the Alby and for that matter most of the husbands of most of the wives of Weipa. Lorraine's husband is not an executive or even necessarily a specialised worker. Their home would likely have been subsidised by Rio Tinto, who make great efforts to appear family and community friendly, even if the majority of their workforce is fly-in, fly-out (meaning they have homes and families elsewhere, often in cities); a practice that is devastating to community building, not to mention the provision and permanent establishment of essential services to remote outback towns. But I digress. Lorraine's modest housekeeper's salary is enough for the two of them to live in relative comfort, provided they exercise a measure of frugality. Hence the reason she and her blue-collar husband can expect to save such a tidy sum inside of one year.

At $22/hour, the housekeepers of Australia earn approximately 150% more than their North American counterparts. In addition, there are Saturday, Sunday and holiday rates, all of which are mandatory in Australia and require employers to pay as much as double time and a half. It's feasible to clear $500 on a public holiday, approximately the same amount I used to earn in a week as director of a non-profit music school back in Canada. Nice work if you can get it. And you can. No one else wants to do it, after all.

~

The restaurant is another world altogether. Chef is temperamental when he's working the line, though I've heard that's common in the profession. He is fond of rolling his eyes at the slightest provocation, for example, when a customer asks for side of gravy or a ramekin of ketchup (Gasp! I mean *tomato sauce*). He throws daggers with his eyes; like it's *you* whose pathetically maladapted taste buds are so shamefully underdeveloped that you need *tomato sauce* to enjoy the perfectly good meal he has expertly prepared for you with *his own bare hands*. Chef's eyes also speak in invisible italics.

Other days he is inexplicably light of heart, shooting peppercorns through a drinking straw at the wait staff while we punch away at the register and polish glasses on our downtime. Hours later he will bear down on us with unrestrained fury when one of the waitresses makes a mistake on her docket and a steak goes out with french fries and salad instead of mashed potatoes and steamed vegetables. As a rule, that waitress is me. I can almost see the steam shooting from his ears when I poke my nose into the kitchen and ask why the salmon is white and not pink. *"Jesus have mercy, you hopeless banana-brain, it's fucking King Salmon,"* his eyes scream.

In the morning he works himself into a temper when he's asked to make one too many discount staff breakfasts. The good-natured Irish waitress employs the most agreeable tone of voice she can muster to request poached eggs, information she has omitted to include on the docket. He looks up at her, nostrils flaring, and growls, using actual words this time, *"Don't talk to me."* As often as we can manage, we don't.

A new recruit, Leanne, is hired to serve in the restaurant but directly demoted to part-time barmaid and kitchen hand (kitchen-speak for dishwasher) when her presentation and personality are deemed unsuited to the image of the restaurant (meaning she's wearing a few extra kilos and likes to talk sci-fi with the customers). She compensates for an acute lack of confidence with over-the-top gestures and, ironically, garish displays of over-confidence. She wears audacious polka dotted sailor dresses with big white collars, her enormous breasts protruding out so far they seem to invade your personal space. In her hair, she ties a colossal bow, like the one your mother might have dressed you in before sending you off to school on your sixth birthday. On Leanne, it has this effect of making her look like a saucy, oversized Christmas present. Early in the evening of her inaugural night on the town with the staff, she tosses a drink at Suvi, the quiet, Finnish chef, soaking her paper-thin frock, and then, inexplicably, calls her a slut. As retribution, she is abandoned at some country pub in the middle of the night. Left to fend for herself, she finds refuge in the home of an elderly Indian gentleman who lives across the road. On his couch or as his lover? The details are unclear but Leanne has undeniably started things off with a bang.

She makes no bones about treating anyone who will listen to an hour-long discourse on the latest television incarnation of Sherlock Holmes, the varied inauthenticities of Australian Comic-Con, and the sci-fi writers she met last year in England. Mid-shift, she will plunk herself down in an empty chair and shoot the breeze with the customers for a solid twenty minutes while the rest of the staff run in circles trying to compensate for her lackadaisical work ethic. When the owner of that once empty chair comes back from his bathroom break, she will jabber on unhindered, oblivious to the bewildered customer who is looking around in confusion, startled by this rather tarty, rotund barmaid who is sitting in his place, before eventually sauntering of to procure himself another chair. She has a habit of saying delightfully inappropriate things that make you want to crawl under your chair, shrink into a tiny, invisible thing, and scurry out the back door. She's looking for a man one night and I say to her, *"Why not Irvine over there? He's seems alright, handsome too."* Leanne looks me square in the face and, without a hint of irony, says, *"Ugh, black people smell."*

Leanne is especially gregarious with the opposite sex and will not hesitate to make advances on the handsomest man in the room, even after he's politely rejected her several times. It's difficult to say whether these quixotic meanderings are all for show or if she is truly that optimistic about the likelihood of success. Either way, Leanne has true grit and despite her unpopularity the other employees cannot help but give her credit for this. Unsurprisingly, her employment here comes to a screeching halt after three short weeks when she is abruptly terminated for something so insignificant that, just one week later, none of us will even remember what it was exactly. Given the enormous expense of coming out here and the pitiful number hours Leanne has been accorded, we can't help but feel compassion for her and even miss her scandalous performances when she is gone. We'll later discover that Leanne is only the first casualty in what quickly escalates to an all-out war between employer and employees. Enter the new General Manager and the beginning of a bitter struggle.

~

Albatross Bay has been without a General Manager since I arrived. It's a well-known fact that the Acting GM sleeps in his office and eats as many as six meals every day at the restaurant's expense. The resort appears to be running fine despite his laziness. It's clean and efficient; on the surface of things, it appears to be running smoothly. And yet things are about to change in a big way.

Several days after the new GM arrives, all managers are called to a secret meeting. Understandably, the GM's ultimate mission will be to cut costs and raise profits. Her point of departure will be to slash the hours of all but essential staff members. Not only will hours be cut so drastically that it will no longer make sense for any paltry underlings to remain, but their environment will be made so inhospitable that it would be too uncomfortable for them to stay even on the off chance that they should wish such a thing. When the bulk of them resign, a few salaried workers on very specific contracts will replace them; the resort will then be able to demand up to seventy hours per week without having to pay for overtime.

For most of us it is undoubtedly a sacrifice to live in Weipa. Apart from the greener-than-green landscapes and shocking red dirt, there is little to see and even less to do. Boozing is the primary activity of choice, though it's a stretch to call it "choice." It is in turns blistering hot and gushing rain. The sun is so painfully scorching that hardly anyone but the aboriginals and a few courageous white people, undoubtedly locals, will venture out of doors after ten in the morning. Those of us who are here are here to work. Not to go fishing, though there's a lot of that and the barramundi are plentiful, not to chase crocodiles and certainly not to stay up until 6:00 a.m. drinking vodka squash. You can do that anywhere. We're here to work. If the work dried up, there'd be no reason to stay.

Many of the staff boarded three or even four separate aircrafts to arrive here, often at great expense. They've given up partners and jobs and apartments to live in pint-sized, aging dongas in the middle of nowhere. Some are backpackers with few worldly possessions and only the basest of needs, but the majority are ordinary Australians gambling on the promise of big money in a remote region where manpower is scant and the need is (relatively) great.

As planned, employees begin dropping like flies when the hours are cut. Many are outright fired, often for the most mundane of reasons, as was the case for Leanne. The night manager allegedly hits his girlfriend late one night after a big evening on the sauce and is given twenty-four hours to evacuate the premises. It's not that I sympathise with the apprentice wife-beater, but for starters, I fail to see how it is his employer's business, and secondly, there are varying reports of what actually happened. He may well have simply smashed a few holes in the wall. Maybe I am being naïve but he just doesn't seem the type. Not surprisingly, it comes out later that his head was on the chopping block already; the big boss was only waiting for her moment to strike.

Rent is raised by more than 50% to $150/week. Even by city standards, this is no bargain. But when you are living in a mouldy chamber not much bigger than a closet with twenty-five-year-old linoleum floors and hardly enough room for your creaky twin bed, it feels like highway robbery. Every day new memos are passed around, full of menacing underlining, highlighting and dreadful italics.

Please take note that staff is entitled to free post-mix and nothing else.

The appearance of the dining room during non-service hours is very ordinary, please pick up the chewed straws and shredded napkins as you leave.

All staff is now required to arrive ten minutes before your shift begins. All non-management staff must now pay for coffee, <u>no exceptions.</u>

Please take note that staff is no longer allowed to order food during service hours.

Staff accommodation will now be inspected for cleanliness twice per month.

All staff is forthwith required to donate one vital organ for use by the resort where it sees fit.

Presumably we are still allowed to order food during non-service hours when there is, *ahem*, no service, no staff, and the kitchen is closed. I am allowed more lenience since my new boyfriend is an actual guest here and his employer spends hundreds of thousands per year on accommodation. In general though, employees are made to feel unwelcome in all common areas other than the bar, where the resort is happy to let us spend our hard-earned dollars.

Evidently, we are expected to freely give ten minutes of our time to our employer since hours are paid by the quarter and not the sixth. What's more, the extra ten minutes are only necessary because lunchtime service hours have also been slashed, resulting in a ten-man pile-up at the register long before the arrival of the poor sod who's been assigned to lunch duty. I will abstain from elaborating further at the risk of discrediting myself by revealing the point to which I am disgruntled by my employer. Suffice to say that discussion of the aforementioned memos quickly usurps boozing as the primary activity of choice for the employees at Albatross Bay, or maybe it's just an extension of it, since bitching and excessive drinking go together like peas and carrots.

The backpackers are the first to bail. They were leaving anyway; why not push up their departure by a few weeks? After that it's the supervisors, incensed when they are demoted to ordinary servers. One by one, the duty managers start to drop off, at which point the formerly top-secret master plan becomes common knowledge, although it isn't nearly as explosive as it might have been since almost all of the underlings have already moved on. And so it trickles down, like a big roof blowing off shingle by shingle, until even Marta starts to talk of applying for a position driving trucks for Rio Tinto. At twenty-two years of service, Marta has been here longer than all of these employees combined. In reward for her efforts, she has been told she is no longer entitled to a sandwich at lunchtime — a flavourless, white-bread-and-salami, two-penny sandwich.

For a time, restaurant service is shoddy and confused. There isn't nearly enough staff to handle the growing clientele. A new duty manager is brought in from Brisbane and firmly establishes himself as the most disagreeable man on earth. Comparable in spirit to Jane the new GM, he has none of her grace or tact and makes the few employees that are left feel like worthless leeches, attempting to re-educate us on basic tasks such as sweeping and mopping. The restaurant is suddenly short of forks and when no replacements are delivered for weeks, I can't help but imagine the GM crunching numbers in her office, thinking to herself; they have hands, don't they? Might as well use them.

~

The price of drinks and meals is raised by at least twenty-five percent, furthering the divide between the restaurant, unmistakably catering to the wealthier white people in town, and the pub, just as obviously catering to the indigenous population.

The indigenous are visibly uncomfortable when they come into the restaurant and quickly make it clear they are only there to make a telephone call or to use the ATM. They sneak out as quickly they came. Is it just a case of people doing what they like to do where they like to do it? Either way, it's hard to ignore when the white people are drinking swanky bottles of wine and munching on one kilo T-bone steaks while thirty-five metres away the aboriginals are drinking three dollar pots of watery beer and funnelling their money into pokey machines in a room that smells like pee and is lit with ugly halogen bulbs – a place the GM's own husband, when he is drunk (which is often enough), refers to as "the pig pen."

Despite his unnervingly casual brand of racism, Jane's husband John is good-natured and sweet. Many evenings he will show up at the pub, heavily intoxicated, and sit around shooting the breeze with the cooks, until his wife shows up and drags him home. Where all of Jane's edges are sharp, all of John's are soft. They come to the restaurant together a few times week, Jane and John. Jane sits texting on her phone through the whole meal while John drinks Extra Dry and stares off into the distance. I always slow down when I walk past their table, ears open, wondering what the two of them could possibly have to talk about. As much as the staff members dislike their new manager, they love her husband by equal amounts.

John's son also works at the Alby. He's younger than me and like his father is prone to making off-handed racist comments without so much as a blink of the eye. The way the word "nigger" rolls off his tongue, you can tell he says it all the time. I never know what to say. A young person in Canada from a middle class background does not go around calling other people niggers. I don't know how to react. Sometimes I actually nod along like I know exactly what he is talking about. It's shameful but it's the only thing I can think to do.

Racism is common enough in Weipa. Because the indigenous are the beneficiaries of endless government handouts; free education, inflated government assistance, tax exemptions, etc., people feel justified in speaking of them in any way they choose. Even though I hear it every day, it still gives me a jolt when Darlene talks about the "dark people." Is that like saying "black people?" Even if Darlene is the last person on earth you would accuse of being racist, she still uses long-antiquated expressions like "half-caste" or "quarter-caste" when referring to certain people she knows. What it's meant to add to the story is unclear to me. This is the way Darlene's experience and culture have taught her to refer to these people. Evidently, it means something to her.

The situation of aboriginals is plain as day out here. To my knowledge, there isn't a single one living at the resort, nor have I seen any working in the shops. Many Weipa businesses like to boast about the number of aboriginals they employ but the people who live here know that this is little more than a publicity campaign. Once per week, the indigenous receive a lump sum payment from Rio Tinto for the use of their lands but a good portion of the money is siphoned through various channels back into the hands of its purveyor. The pubs are often packed to the rafters and most of their money is spent before the weekend is out. A good portion of it goes into the beer taps but a much greater chunk goes into the "pokies" – an innocent enough sounding name when compared to the more lecherous American term, "slots." Although 85% of the astounding revenue from these machines (easily ten thousand on a slow day) goes back to the government, even the paltry leftovers represent tens of thousands in profit for the resort. And so it goes, round and round like a carousel where everyone seems to profit but the indigenous people themselves.

It's futile to try and allocate blame. After all, I'm only an outsider calling it like she sees it. There is a whole universe of activity going on here that I know nothing about. Nor would I pronounce myself fundamentally against the mining industry. Far from it. Rio Tinto provides well-paying jobs for twenty thousand Australians and at least half that many Canadians. The women I work with have great lives. Their children get scholarships from Rio. Their homes are paid for. They travel often and lack for nothing. The mining boom won't last forever and, as far as I can see, the Alby is only striking while the iron is hot.

As for me, I try and exercise gratitude for everyday I spend here and every dollar I make. Had the new GM been in place when I applied, I never would have been offered the job. I had no hospitality experience on my resume and actually talked myself up for having cleaned my mother's Bed & Breakfast as a pre-teen. Even a few weeks in, all signs pointed to my being an untrainable waste of money. To be fair, Jane has never been anything but kind to me. No matter how many awful stories I hear about her, I can't help but like her. It's true that I don't get the same hours anymore. Mine have been slashed as much as anyone else's. And yet here I am, three months later, a few thousand dollars in the black and a shiny new lover on my arm. It's a bigger payout than any I could have imagined.

Birds of a Feather

In the early days Matthew and I often spoke of marriage, so amped up were we on the ecstasy of our emotions, so swept away in the weather of each other. It must have been mostly hypothetical, a vain attempt at communicating the magnitude of our feelings for one another. All rationality would abandon us; washed away in the pure bliss of new love, and the temptation to make a baby right then and there would be almost palpable. I don't mean "baby making" as a euphemism for sex either — I mean getting right down to the delicate business of conceiving a child. Had Matthew signed his divorce papers before leaving for Weipa, God knows we probably would have gone down to the St. Luke Uniting and Anglican Co-operating Parish and come back to Sydney married and pregnant with twins.

Day by day we twisted our heads back on, learned to walk and talk again under the weight of the enormous growth in our hearts. And as the ability to think rationality returned to us, Matt began to feel somewhat burdened by the tonnage of things that were said, and pulled me aside one day to explain that maybe, just maybe, he might not be exactly ready for marriage just yet. This was hardly shocking to me and had I been thinking more clearly wouldn't even have been particularly painful to hear. I've been saying for years that marriage doesn't really matter to me.

And yet no matter how unreasonable or illogical this may sound, I'd still like my partner to want to marry me.

By the time we got around to having that conversation, Matt and I had been living in a hotel room for more than three months and become close enough to do and say almost anything in the company of each other. While our romance was still very much alive, I'd never been so comfortable with anyone in my life and the reality of knowing another's strange quirks and nasty habits to such a degree has put me in a good position to reflect on my single life, not without a bit of nostalgia, and contrast it with my current situation as half of a whole.

~

Before embracing full-time conjugality in a hotel room in far north Queensland, I had lived alone in Montreal for a period just shy of ten years. Though intermittently obliged to answer to the occasional boyfriend or pseudo-partner over the years, my time, money, and resources were more or less my own, to dispose of where and when I saw fit, without reproach or remorse whatsoever the self-seeking course of action I might have chosen to embark upon. If I felt like living in squalor amid a month's worth of soiled laundry piled on every available surface, well then I would live in squalor and savour every disgusting second of it. If I felt like blasting *Das Moldau* at eight o'clock in the morning or failed to change the kitty litter two days in a row, there were only the neighbours to contend with. There would be no one around to judge me if I spent a week in my pyjamas playing *Donkey Kong* until I was near blind. When I decided I needed three rooms to myself and moved to a neighbourhood where the majority of locals lived on government money that they boozed away outside the *Dunkin' Donuts* from dawn until dusk, nobody asked for explanations or justification, or even pointed out the obvious irony of such misplaced indulgence.

I loved being a single woman. Even allowing for the perpetual risk the occasional Saturday night alone, there was always the delicious aroma of possibility, the simple certainty that anything could happen. Alone on your sofa lounge, you are free to skip the continent for a week or two, contemplate a career in war journalism, or chuck it all in and study the violin, without any dreadful voice of reason echoing noisily in your ear. Not that anyone does these things of course, but you can if you want to, and that's the point.

All of the really gritty and interesting characters in *On the Road* were steadfastly single, even in love. Ed Dunkel only married Galatea in the hope she would fund their adventures and then abandoned her somewhere in Arizona when she refused to cooperate. Even when Sal Paradise and Terry were sleeping in that country barn somewhere in Mexico, looking up at the moon and at the spiders spinning webs above their heads, basking in the warmth of their love, it was clear that Sal would leave her just as soon as the season changed, singledom being so fundamental to the Kerouacian plot, evoking images of young Japhys leaping from rock to rock, the ultimate goal of which is merely to arrive at a clearer definition of self and identity. The women don't even get last names in those stories — Terry, Marylou, Camille — all minor characters, further evidence of the inherent uselessness of the couple to these young free spirits.

On the other hand coupledom is, as one journalist aptly dubbed it, "a contract in the joint management of a mundane existence." It means getting uncomfortably familiar with your partner's intestinal eccentricities. It means chitchatting away beside them while they clip their toenails or inspect some anomalous lump on a part of your body you are no longer (or never were) able to get a good look at. It is loving someone in their sweatpants and caring for them when they get sick. It's little things, big things, gross things, and beautiful things.

This marriage business though, is sticky stuff. I hardly know anyone who isn't confused about it. Is it still relevant to the times? Why do we still cling to it when it appears to mean so very little? Is it media pressure? Is it the work of the wedding industry, a seventy billion dollar a year business in the US? Or is it Beyoncé's fault, with all the "put a ring on it" business?

Being raised in the family that I was, getting married was important. Many of my siblings submitted to stern lectures and damnations from my father when it came out that their de facto spouse had fallen pregnant. Soon after they would marry — a process the Brethren call "making it right is the eyes of the Lord."

When I moved, albeit briefly, into my boyfriend's apartment sometime before my nineteenth birthday, I continued to refer to him as my "roommate" in front of my father and even went out of my way to stress that we slept in separate bedrooms — a barefaced and unnecessary lie. My father would never have asked questions about something like that. But I've been speaking in half-truths to my Dad for years, carefully constructing a more religiously correct version of myself. It's second nature to me. He still calls me *Pinky* and takes me for quarter chicken dinners at Swiss Chalet. If I ever decided to marry, it would probably be more for his benefit than my spouse's.

Marriage is scary. And from what I can see, if makes change harder. For a lot of people, it seems to remove the impetus to grow and make life better, for yourself and your partner. Or maybe that's just the way I see it, because I know it's not for me. Matthew is definitely scared — and sensible, much as I might have it otherwise — and rightfully so being that his marriage actual did end up a worst-case scenario.

He wants to take things slowly and that's fine by me. But it seems almost daily that I am trying to sway him from his fixation with *the reality of things*, which is actually just a catch-all phrase for every bad thing that could happen to us. It's possible we'll make each other unhappy; perhaps we will bicker and cause each other pain. His girls may not like me and I'll be a pariah in their once-comfortable home. It actually takes me some effort to come up with these disaster scenarios. They are futile by my assessment since it's equally possible we will make each other blissfully happy, that I will end up a regular fixture in a happy home.

I have less and less use for realism, anyway. I've read too many novels. It's come to my attention that I'm not a very realistic person — nor was my recent flirtation with realism by way of law school an especially propitious endeavour. I spend an unseemly amount of time thinking about who will play in the hypothetical movie version of my life or how I will work off all the pastries I plan to eat on my hypothetical European book tour. Rarely does the risk of losing everything in an expensive divorce cross my mind — but then maybe those kinds of fears come as a sort of addendum to your first mortgage payment, new car, or purebred German shepherd.

The best things about a heart multiplied by two don't necessarily look great on paper, but perhaps coupledom's very unglamourousness is also its primary selling point. It has no glossy coating; it is simply tried, tested, and true. It is memorising every line and every grain in the face of your lover. It is sleeping every night in the arms of someone whose looks, smells, and sounds are comforting and familiar, even in the dark.

It is someone who helps, someone who understands things about you that you don't understand about yourself. It is coming home to someone who will listen and nod and look for things in your eyes that aren't coming out in your words. It is the smell of food that you didn't prepare yourself, wafting up through the hallway after a long day. It is someone in the wings saying "I'll back you up" and that feeling you get when that someone looks at you in a way that no one else does.

In my case, it is the nest of blond curls that run smooth as silk through my fingers. It is the way Matthew studies my face while I am watching television or reading a book. It is driving back to the hotel just as the sun is beginning to set, a bottle of wine and a paper bag full of steaming take-out containers in my lap, Neil Diamond blasting on the radio as we sing at the top of our lungs, *"She got the way to move me, Cherry, she got the way!"* It is the magic moments between working, sleeping and eating. Sometimes, just sometimes, it is also having someone to blame when life is not perfect. It is the man that gives me love and compassion and refuses to let me quit my job. It is the nights we fall asleep too tired for even a few minutes of quiet conversation, and yet keep waking up and rolling toward the other to say I love you before turning over and falling back into sleep.

For all the glamour of singledom, the things I miss the most are easily reproduced inside a relationship. When I think of the late nights on the town, it's the company of the wonderful women in my life that I crave the most and not the thrill of being young and unattached, the quiet mornings out on the porch with a steaming cup of tea and a bit of sunlight for company.

Being single isn't all peaches and cream either. Often it means choosing between bad sex or no sex, bad dates or no dates. And what about the late nights reading *Cosmopolitan* articles about deadbeat husbands, full of foreboding subtext that you could be their next victim? And is there any agony like new love, whiling away the hours analyzing the smallest of gestures, long forgotten by the object of your amour? Writing off relationships because they can be unpredictable and tricky to navigate would be like writing off childbearing because of annoying PTA meetings. There's too much good to paint over with bad.

~

It would be dishonest not to admit that I am hardly qualified to have an opinion about such matters, having never been married or even lived with a man for any significant period of time. Moreover, this entire conversation was spawned by another conversation in which my lover rather suddenly and forcefully eschewed marriage, so you could hardly call any of this an unbiased disquisition. Either I am prematurely mounting my defence in the event that we decide not to marry, or the pundits are in fact right and the state of unmarriage actually is reserved for lonely and dejected spinsters.

In any case, all these pretty philosophies blow away in the wind when the heart meets with the object of its desire. The reason is that, objectively speaking, you may be able to say what you want and don't want from the opposite sex (and for that matter, the same sex) but subjectively, you can never know what you might want from any individual person. A host of overlapping emotions come into play and the once-predictable heart will counteract with a plethora of external factors. Maybe you need to get it down on paper in order to be convinced of the velocity of your lover's commitment. Maybe there are legal or geographical reasons that justify marriage, or children to consider.

How do you know how much or what kind of love is necessary to justify marriage? Which is the love that lasts and which is the love where you learn your lessons and move on? As Jane Austen wrote, "There are as many forms of love as there are moments in time." Sometimes love is no more than the meeting of two people with similar ideas about the nature of love, a similar desire to love and be loved in a certain way. Sometimes it is as simple as being treated the way we feel we ought to be treated and appreciated for the things we feel we ought to be appreciated for.

It seems no one really knows anything definitive about love and marriage, even when we are caught up in the thick of it. For the most part, you just have to feel your way through, improvising where necessary. When your partner says maybe he doesn't want to marry you right this minute, it's important to ask yourself whether or not you actually wanted that in the first place. Having had some experience with divorced men (and, incidentally, with men who claimed to be divorced), I'd say it would be prudent to give them a bit of extra leeway on the subject. Often all this fixation on where a relationship is going and where the last one led only serves to distract us from the here and now, from taking a good survey of the present state of affairs and saying, okay, *this* here is good, *this* is comfortable, *this* moment makes me happy today.

Bye, Bye, Birdies

15 March 2012

Concerned parties of the Albatross Bay Resort,

It is with some regret that I tender my resignation at such a respectable establishment as yours, effective the 24th of March 2012. I will take this opportunity to thank the resort for the excellent training and sizable paycheques that I have been provided with over the last four months.

Hither I go in pursuit of love and adventure in Sydney, the magnificent capital city of New South Wales, where I will commence my new life as suburban stepmother and author of the next great American novel, though not necessarily in that order.

With extensive gratitude and good feelings,

Amy Knapp

~

We're leaving soon. Jane offered to give me a reference before I even had a chance to ask, her assistant manager as well. I've had my fill of mixing drinks and cleaning toilets, so I hope I won't have to use them. The situation at the resort continues to devolve. Somehow the boss lady has come to know that one of the chefs is taking medication for depression. She's been accused of calling him "delusional," rather than acknowledging his condition. Though I can't substantiate this claim, we've all read the signs posted in the bar, the bistro, and the bottle shop forbidding any staff members to sell or otherwise provide him with alcohol. One of the new salaried workers, Stuart, confesses over dinner than he's just put in seventeen hours of unpaid overtime. Even so, Jane has also posted a sign in the bar specifying that Stuart specifically is entitled to no more than one glass of post-mix per day. It's the insult to end all insults; a glass of post-mix is worth less than five cents.

Footie season has started so Matthew is now glued to the television Friday through Monday. It's a side effect of dating in Australian that no one tells you about. The men are very burly and handsome but it can be difficult to hold their attention; rugby league is a cruel mistress. Having an Australian partner means you are essentially single eight months a year. Short of dancing around naked in front of the television, there's not much you can do. For the right team, not even a lurid striptease will get you very far. That's rugby love.

Slowly I am learning to differentiate the multitude of sports referred to by the blanket term "footie." Given they are all referred to by the same name, it's surprising how vehemently Matthew insists on their being completely different sports. It's like anything; the more you love it, the more you defend its complexity, the finite differences that make it special. As it is, fewer scrums and restrictions on forward passing mean very little to me. However, I have noticed the shortness of the shorts worn by those in the AFL. The way I see it, AFL, rugby league, and rugby union are sort of like the mini-skirt, the bubble-skirt, and the pencil-skirt; to Matthew, they're just skirts, but to me, they're very specific looks with very specific functions. The rules are completely different.

No one can actually explain to me what makes AFL such a lame sport, but it's an important rivalry among Australians:

rugby league (NRL) v. AFL. Maybe it's the singlets and short shorts. In New South Wales, they call it GayFL, openly mocking the misguided fools who enjoy this sport. For fans of NRL, AFL is an assault on the purity of the sport. Both sides insist theirs is the sport played by "real men." In any case, the subtleties of the sport are lost on me. In my family, we played piano. We were gangly kids and our parents weren't the sporting type; sports were too worldly, I suppose.

Since the television is monopolised now, I go up to the pub more often, mostly to attend a steady train of farewell parties. Staff are dropping off so fast, I can hardly keep up with them. We've had so many send-offs it's getting to be a running joke. By now there are only three or four left who have been here since the beginning. Although sometimes after a big night of long speeches and too many farewell shots, when we are all standing arm in arm, saturated in booze at 3:00 a.m. and swaying to the music, singing yet another run of *The Gambler*, I get the sense that I will miss this place. I'm itching to get out, but just like Hervey Bay, I can already sense nostalgia creeping up on me. The history of my adventures in Weipa is already rewriting itself in shades of sentiment, coloured with the cool melodies of Kenny Rogers.

~

Matthew has invited me back to Sydney, where we will live with one half of his twin teenagers in his rented suburban townhouse. He's got to go home eventually, and he can't go on extending his contract forever, nor would I wish him to. We worked all this out months ago but now that the time is come to test out our relationship in a place Matt calls "the real world," he's losing his hair, his sleep, and his marbles worrying about it. For Matthew,

Weipa is an alternate universe where he has no kids, no estranged wife, no mother, and no responsibilities. Sydney is the real deal.

The difference is that, for me, this whole country is an alternate universe. For that matter, the life we are living is a total aberration. I'm still waiting for someone to jump out of the woodwork, slap me on the back and yell, "*Gotcha!*" I still sometimes think I might wake up in Montreal, forty-five minutes before my Torts class and find this was all a dream. I have completely lost my grip on "reality." I've travelled so far from the things I once considered "real" that the word has no meaning for me anymore. It's my belief that you just choose the thing you want your life to be and then call that reality. You look at what *is* and, if you like it, you call that reality. You look at the man sleeping beside you and, if you like what you see in his heart, you call him a *real* man.

I don't know what's coming, where I'm going, or how I will feel when I get there. I'm just going to stick my hands out in front of me and feel my way ahead. I'm going to Sydney, and I have a feeling it's going to be good for both of us. If it's not great, we'll find a way to make it so. We're two now; we're in this together. We can help each other. And a bird in hand is worth two in the bush, as they say.

~

"How did you come into my life?"
"Magic."
"I'm being serious."
"So am I."

PART THREE

THE SUBURBS, NEW SOUTH WALES

Faith Is a Bird that Feels the Dawn Approach and Sings in the Dark

Sydney Harbour is like a photograph of itself: old-time ferry boats teeming with Asian tourists snapping pictures on oversized cameras, cobblestone walkways swarming with tour vendors and dealers in nostalgic paraphernalia, and the astounding views across the harbour. Looking out across the harbour, the Opera House stands so majestic the mere sight of it is like a punch in the gut. It's no wonder there are so many people. The combined effect of all this, punctuated by the stately Harbour Bridge, makes you feel like a real world traveller, like you're somewhere, at long last.

I snap some photos for posterity and move on to my real mission, which is to catch up on all the shopping I missed out on in Weipa, where there was only one clothing store that sold mostly fishing shirts and baby jumpers. The only spending I've been able to manage in the last three months has been at the local Woolworth's: litre bottles of V8 juice, rice crackers, the occasional *Cosmopolitan* magazine, and way too many gummy worms. I've been itching to spend some of that hard earned, toilet-cleaning cash and downtown Sydney seems like just the place for scratching. Even knowing Matt will jump on the occasion to mock me for it later, I head straight for David Jones on Elizabeth Street, a high-fashion wonderland sadly reserved for the select few dowdy, middle-aged ladies who can afford it. The Australian equivalent of Holt Renfrew or Ogilvy's, David Jones is an incomparable specimen of a truly great department store: timeless, elegant, classic. Like many a department store of its kind, the ground floor is a glowing, pristine, whiter than white landscape. Enormous pseudo-Grecian white columns sealed with elegant, Victorian crown mouldings support 40-foot ceilings. An elderly man plays Mendelssohn on a full sized Steinway & Sons grand piano.

It feels so much like Christmas that I have to take a moment to calculate backward and forward before concluding that, while it isn't in fact Christmas, at David Jones a similar variety of seasonal warmth has been carefully crafted to filter through the store three hundred and sixty five days a year.

Without little regard for price tags and even less for hypothetical budgeting, I wander through a dizzying field of luxury merchandise, run my fingers over the finest calf skin designer purses, rub a $300 silk scarf the size of a tissue against my cheek, delight in the crisp white shirts of Tom Ford or a pair of glossy Armani gumboots, savouring the luxurious textures, inhaling the sweet smell of factory-fresh rubber.

Predictably, the store clerks are uniformly snot-nosed and bad-tempered, perhaps because they were born this way but more likely because they have noted my faded jeggings, my way-too-comfortable running shoes and my $5 polyester dress. I should be annoyed but somehow it makes this place that much more perfect. It's tempting to put on an affected English accent and demand four different sizes in six styles of polished suede Jimmy Choos at $2500 a pop. I don't actually do things like that though, not even on the other side of the world. On the way out I walk extra slow past the bargain bin and hope no one notices me looking.

Despite having purchased an all-day transit pass for the express purpose of seeing as many neighbourhoods as possible in one afternoon, the train has unfortunately deposited me in a shoppers Mecca from which I am unable to extract myself. With no map, no information or sense of direction, dumb luck leads me to the Strand Arcade, a three-story affair so delicately majestic and detailed that I am afraid to take photos, rationalising that if cameras are forbidden at the Musée d'Orsay, surely they are also forbidden here.

The Strand is a dazzling Victorian shopping arcade built in 1892; one of the last of its kind. Impossibly intricate ironwork brackets and carved hardwood railings decorate the narrow galleries. Red cedar wood glows in the sunlight, which pours in through the arching glass rooftop. There must be an elevator somewhere but common practice seems to dictate use of the stairs, which are elegantly decked out in solid cedar balustrades and metres of colourful stained glass windows. From the balconies of the second and third floors, you get the full effect of the elaborately tiled floor, so catholic in detail it makes me wonder if this building wasn't a church in some former incarnation (it wasn't) — at least that would explain the stained glass windows and humbling deistic presence you feel in this place. The arcade is a work of art, nay, even a work of philosophy. The jeweller on the second floor has placed a sign in his window, a translation from the Latin; *Faith is a bird that feels dawn breaking and sings while it is still dark* — I like to think this was the motto of the building's architect as he was drew up the blueprint.

As if to seal in concrete the perfection of this construction, the most famous of the merchants at Strand Arcade is Strand Hatters on the ground floor, a nice old-fashioned hat shop for men. It's understated and even quaint, staffed with three spectacularly cool yet not *too* handsome young men, smartly dressed in casual chequered shirts, complete with sweater vest and college loafers. They are laughing, of course, carrying on light conversion amongst themselves and the occasional patron. Rather than feeling excluded from their uber fashionable party of three, or wishing if only you could belong to this exclusive and chic fraternity of hat-wearers, you get the feeling of fitting right in alongside them, like you might just buy yourself a nice flat white coffee, have your shoes shined, then sit and admire the scenery for the rest of the day.

The Strand is almost entirely dedicated to Australian artisans and designers, the notion of buying local being more all-pervasive in Australia than any country I have visited. Australians are a proud people, endeared with an honest sort of patriotism that American governments have been clamouring to manufacture for the last century. Even at the grocery store, it seems like every second product has a *Made in Australia* seal, while the rest are labelled more cryptically *Processed in Australia from Local and Imported Ingredients*. It appears manufacturers are getting hip to this trend and looking for ways to exploit it.

Similarly, many formerly made in Australia clothing brands are now assembling their wares in China or Bangladesh. Brands that have built solid reputations as proudly Australian are moving production overseas while continuing to capitalise on their Australian-ness and consumers' mistaken belief in what actually constitutes "local." That's part of what makes the Strand so magic. It's full Australiana everywhere, handmade by local artisans from locally sourced materials. Many of the stores are half-shop, half-studio. Often the woman behind the counter turns out to be the artist herself.

Dragging myself from the Strand — a buffet of the senses — I happen upon the Queen Victoria building, which, even outside of its architectural grandeur, would almost certainly have been an attraction for me by name alone. Similarly decorative flooring abounds, though the stores here are a combination of local and international brands, the common thread being fancy and exorbitantly priced. It is in the so-called bargain basement of this building that willpower finally abandons me in the face of what appear to be real bargains, at least in contrast to the $1800 leather purses of the first floor. I exit the store with a double-bagged load of kitchen wares: from butcher knife to cheese grater to polished wood chopping block. Fortunately for my now depleted bank account, the weight of these purchases demands I return home directly.

~

Back at the suburban homestead, I've been rearranging drawers and cupboards for days. Subtly I hope, since Matthew and his daughters have been here forever and they have what he calls "systems." I don't wish to develop a reputation as an intruder, or worse, as the wicked stepmother, so I keep my mouth shut about the "system" of storing dirty laundry in the bathtub and instead place baskets in everyone's closet in the vain hope that they can take a hint. The house is comfortable and sparsely decorated. It is almost entirely free of clutter, the bulk of which is contained in two or three discreet locations throughout the house. Even so, for several nights I lie awake for hours stewing about the loose paper scraps in the junk drawer and the mountain of unidentified bits and bobbles in the garage. One particularly restless afternoon, I throw open the garage door and clean the entire thing, top to bottom, dusting, sorting, rearranging, vacuuming, and stacking. I feel a satisfaction so complete that I have to go in and out every thirty minutes for the rest of the day, admiring the result of my handiwork.

There's probably some primal behaviour happening here. I need to feel like I live here too. Matt calls it nesting, which annoys me because it threatens my independence. I need a room of my own: a place that feels like my own. Mentally I've already carved out a corner of this garage for myself. I have a dream of covering the concrete walls in stripy wallpaper, setting up a refurbished wooden desk, possibly salvaged from someone else's garage and finished off with a lamp draped with an old scarf to give the room a soft glow. The room would be complete with an antique chair — the kind you might have seen behind the desk of an Oxford professor in the seventies.

I have ideas about maintaining one's private space and sense of self even after life deals you a permanent cast of characters. A rooms of one's own and all that. Matt doesn't understand this. While I was reading Virginia Woolf in college, he was raising kids. He believes that I think this way because I haven't had children yet, that I don't know what it's like to sacrifice. Maybe he's right. Either way, the idea makes my stomach turn. I'm not ready to surrender my independence.

The house is full of empty nooks and crannies hinting at the absence of an armoire or aquarium. The couch has no pillows, a TV stand sits empty, serving no other purpose than to indicate the presence of nothing where once was something. Half of the house has long since been emptied of its treasures. It's full of empty corners where once were the personal possessions of a loved one. The other half of that loved one, so deeply buried was he in his misery, has neglected to spread out his own things and fill in the empty spaces. Perhaps there were remnants left behind, perhaps the spaces were not so very bare as they are now; I suspect his mother may have removed the last traces of Matthew's estranged wife, out of kindness to me.

I am reminded of my own mother, who also moved into a ready-made home on the occasion of her marriage, complete with its own pre-established systems and rebellious teenagers. No similar kindness was afforded my mother upon taking up residence with my father after the death of his first wife, Doris. The closets and cupboards had been left teeming with the deceased woman's clothing and personal effects. Toward the end of her life Doris' mind had deserted her, or so the story goes, and for an entire year leading up to her eventual suicide, she drank only black coffee and ate nothing but raw pasta. When she finally related the story to me, my mother had tears in her eyes as she explained how Doris' drawers were still rattling with dried macaroni.

So I putter around the house cleaning out drawers, ironing in front of the TV (prematurely observing a house "system"), baking cookies, boiling a kilo of brown rice for no good reason other than that I can: I don't live in a hotel room anymore. I have a real house with a stove and everything.

Essentially, I am waiting for this new life to begin. I flew in four days early, though I have forgotten why exactly, maybe to get a jump on some of those systems Matt's been teaching me. He was scheduled to arrive this evening and even as his flight is delayed again and again I am still banking on his swift return to my waiting arms. His teenage daughters will arrive tomorrow, one to visit and one to stay. I'm nervous and unprepared, but like the bird that feels the dawn beginning to break, I'll just go ahead and start singing in the dark.

Livin' in the Sprawl

When you live as a family, you have to tell them where you are going and what time you'll be back. After you put your make-up on, you have to screw all the lids back on and put everything back in the drawer. When planning a family meal, you have to clear it with them — if you expect them to eat it. In Australia (for that matter, in almost any place other than my apartment back home and possibly Africa), plain rice and zucchini does not constitute a main course. These are the sorts of things you have to learn when you plant yourself smack in the middle of someone else's suburban family after living alone for ten years.

Inserting yourself into someone else's life can be tricky; they have their own habits and their own ideas about the "correct" way of doing things. When you start your own family, you decide together where to store the cups and saucers or determine the best method for dealing with tax invoices. Life evolves naturally into a place where everyone is comfortable. If there is mess, it's because you have collectively decided the precise state of untidiness with which all parties are comfortable. Introduce a new person and everything goes awry; suddenly it's unclear who gets the best spot on the couch, who is responsible for taking out the garbage, or who is supposed to do the washing up after dinner. The pecking order that had evolved organically to accommodate the passage of time crumbles and must be re-established from scratch.

And yet it must be equally tricky to accommodate this person who is attempting to insert herself into your life. Much as you want to make her comfortable, things were running pretty smoothly before she came along and now that she's here, nobody knows whether to sit at the table or in front of the TV after dinner has been served. You're watching rugby on Saturday night, the way you have done every Saturday night for the last ten years, and there she is wondering when is the next *commercial* and can't we just watch a few minutes of that *Harry Potter* movie on channel nine?

~

I get a weird kind of pleasure out of being a house mom. It doesn't feel real. It's like a magical game of dress-up — Sim City Stepmother in 3D. Nothing that happens here is anything like my life. I used to arrange the surfaces of my house to accommodate volumes of Dostoyevsky and piles of experimental albums by obscure string bands. Now all the furniture is pointed at the TV. I used to spend long hours alphabetizing my collection of old postcards and listening to Yo-Yo Ma. Now I mostly just watch reality shows and eat junk food.

I'm not allowed to move the furniture. Matthew is finicky about me moving things around; his instinct is to protect that sanctity of the household and the comfort of everyone in it. His daughters, on the other hand, don't seem to care. They've seen their fair share of change this past year; they're masters in the art of rolling with the punches, far more flexible than their father gives them credit for.

The girls are good-spirited and not overly verbal. They while away entire evenings tapping away on their cell phones and clicking at their laptops, intermittently engaging in live conversation, seemingly out of nowhere since no preliminary greetings are ever exchanged. We are eternally mystified by what exactly they are doing, beyond the vague notion that it has something to do with Twitter and the latest boy band of the month.

Teenagers are the most expensive creatures on earth. They are constantly, interminably, asking their father for money; money for the train or in case they get thirsty, money for lunch or a new outfit, the necessity of which is positively life or death. Matt is perpetually doling out bills and never gets any change. Sometimes it is simple necessities like netball fees or a box of tampons, but just as often it is a pair of concert tickets, a GHD hair straightener, or a trip to Melbourne. He takes it all in stride, reproaching them with love and then giving in to their every inclination ninety-nine percent of the time.

The girls are crazy for One Direction. They don't often think of anything else. Their zeal for this shaggy-haired band of boys is insatiable. The precision with which they plan to hunt them down on their Australian tour is reminiscent of a CIA reconnaissance mission. They film music videos, learn elaborate dance routines and coordinate flash mobs, enter contests and make concrete plans for what they will do when they win — not in a when-I-win-the-lottery type of way but with a genuine hopefulness completely lost on adults. The dedication with which they plan their missions is only matched by the dedication with which they try to convince their reluctant father to go along with their elaborate scheming. Rather than getting caught up in the outrageousness of it, as Matt does, the whole thing strikes me as a fairly healthy enterprise, even a little blasé. Don't kids do drugs anymore?

~

It's impossible to know what teenagers like and don't like since they choose their words with such economy. Yet even if they were willing to express their feelings in more than three words, they aren't home enough to critique or complain. In the beginning I tried to use food as a bargaining tool, baking chocolate chip cookies every other day in a poorly disguised bid to make the girls like me. But in the end the things that earn me brownie points with the girls are completely arbitrary, like my Canadian accent, for example, which not only establishes me as exotic and foreign, but also as a distant cousin of Justin Bieber.

There are changes in my day-to-day transactions with Matt. He worries so constantly about our wellbeing, it's a wonder he has any time left to brush his teeth and shave his face. Watching him play the part of the parent, I meet a brand new incarnation of someone I thought I knew inside and out.

Some things change but many of our habits stay the same. The walls of the house have ears now and there is hardly more than a closet separating the bedrooms upstairs, which isn't far off from living in a hotel room. If anything it's a welcome excuse to make love in the afternoons or in some secret corner of the house while the girls are at school.

Life feels remarkably normal, which is funny since it is actually so far from anything I've experienced before. The TV is on all the time and I never get to watch movies anymore because there is always some program the girls absolutely cannot miss, like *Home and Away* or *My Kitchen Rules*, which run at least an hour long and play every single night of the week.

There's a small pleasure that comes with mundanity. I never liked experimental music all that much anyway. I only liked the idea of it. Somehow it's a relief to do things in a predictable way, to not always be blazing a new trail. It's a relief to watch television for hours every day, even if some part of me knows that it's not sustainable. It's a relief to not be studying for anything, practicing anything, or working toward anything, sort of like someone hit the pause button and I just get to hang out for a while, listening to the preprogrammed track.

I fall asleep exhausted and overwhelmed and dream of beautiful music. A year ago today I was thirty pounds lighter and my spirit a million pounds heavier. Every day was a metaphysical heavy-lifting contest, at the end of which I would fall asleep a different kind of exhausted and overwhelmed, dreaming of Pizza Pockets and Big Gulp Slurpees. Who could have foreseen that such a short time later I would be here on the other side of the world, living a life that is the precise opposite of what it was back then? Life has a funny way of throwing you a bone when you least expect it, but you have to be standing at the ready, willing and able to snatch it from the air and claim that bone for yourself.

The Missionary's Wife

"If you believe in the gods, then you believe in the cycle of time that we are all playing our parts in a story that is told again, and again, and again throughout eternity." — Laura Roslin, President of the Twelve Colonies

Anyone who's paying attention would not deny the way history repeats itself. It's also a common theme in sci-fi and fantasy stories; I learned it from *Battlestar Galactica*. ("*All this has happened before and all this will happen again.*") The show itself is hardly more than an updated, more palatable version of the bible; that is, if the disciples were robots and Jesus was a philandering physician called Gaius Baltar.

I consider myself an authority on the bible, compared to my peers, anyway. I know the lines of Matthew, Mark, Luke, and John the same way I know the lines on my own face. As children we read them every day after dinner for upwards of an hour; slumped in our chairs with bellies full of spaghetti, legs twitching impatiently under the table. Those stories are hardly new either; most are a version of some earlier story, wearing the clothes of Christianity. And they're still being retold today, except they're called *Star Wars*, *Lord of the Rings,* or *The Chronicles of Narnia.*

The overarching theme in all of these stories is the same: we are born in light and joy, with time we learn to suffer, suffering blots out the light and we must band together to overcome darkness. Only then can we rise again and finally, in the end (which is also the beginning), be allowed to die. There are the leaders, Jesus, Gandalf, Obi Wan, etc.; there are chosen ones, Frodo, Luke Skywalker, Kara Thrace, Jack Sully; and there are the dark ones; Palpatine, President Snow, the Romulans, and Lord Saruman.

My mother read us a lot of those fantasy stories. We learned about ourselves and about the world as much from *Lord of the Rings* as we did from the bible. And yet the story that interested me the most was her own, a story not so different from the one I am living today. The details are vastly different but the characters are essentially the same; there's the older man character, still reeling from the loss of his wife; there are the hapless teenagers, lost in their private adolescent universe; there is the ghost of another woman, the perfume, the pants suits, and the collection of expired lotions and sprays still hanging around in the backs of drawers; and the empty house where once was a home; the family bewildered and shell-shocked, their heads turning in all directions.

As Gaius Baltar once said, *"when we know what we are, then we can find the truth out about others, seek what they are; the truth about them."* Every time I prepare a tuna casserole, hang the laundry in the yard or pick up a trail of sodden tissues, I am also learning my mother's truth. I imagine her standing out in the garden in her hand-sewn Mennonite get-up, kerchief on her head, hand raised to her forehead and eyes squinting in the sun, wondering if she should or should not tell my father about the half-ounce of marijuana she found under his eldest son's bed, or if his younger son will be out of jail in time for Christmas. Comparatively speaking, I got off easy.

~

Predictably, my parents met at bible study. Because the Brethren did not believe in hierarchy, Thomas Knapp was not officially their leader, but he was the closest thing they had to one. He'd been a missionary for thirty years; perhaps that was why he was deemed worthy. As a leader, he was not without flaws. Though his opinion was respected among his colleagues, his refusal to budge on certain points of doctrine was a constant thorn in their sides, often causing considerable upset at the Brethren's weekly meetings.

Though their meetings took place in Thomas's own living room, Lynda did not converse with him. She had no reason to do so, nor would it have been considered proper. Her brothers enjoyed an easy friendship with Thomas and maintained a healthy respect for him. Given he was nearly fifty and Lynda in her early twenties and only just, they were not an obvious match. No one would have thought of them as such. So it came as some surprise to Lynda when Thomas slipped her a letter (*"All this has happened before ..."*) after one of their Sunday meetings, a letter she accepted discreetly and concealed on her person until she was safely returned to her parent's home.

She had inferred from his mannerisms that the letter was meant to be private, though it was not explicitly stated. She only dared to open the letter after locking herself in the bathroom at her parent's house and wedging a chair under the doorknob. Her hands shook as she unfolded the letter; perhaps some part of her knew that its contents would transform her completely and forever. The letter stated in simple language that Thomas wished for Lynda to be his wife. He explained that he felt he needed her; mentally, spiritually and physically; and that he would accept any children that came from the relationship. Romance, indeed.

Thomas had three children from a previous marriage, two of whom were still at home, barely teenagers. It was known among the Brethren that Thomas's first wife had suffered mental illness and taken her life about six months previously. It was thought that she'd driven to the Niagara Glen and thrown herself into the Gorge, a fact that was eventually confirmed when her body washed up on the American side some three months after her suicide.

At the time of the letter, Thomas's family was still in shock. They were detached from each other, having lost the one member who united them. Religious and moral pressures had alienated him from the children of his first wife the same way they would eventually alienate him from those of his second. (*"All this has happened before and all this will happen again."*) Thomas once said to Lynda that her and her brother meant more to him even than his own family. They were his spiritual family; when it came down to it, they were what mattered most to him.

As she read his letter, Lynda cycled through three distinct emotions; anger, since there was no earthly reason for him to think she might be his wife; laughter, because the whole idea was so ridiculous to her; finally acceptance, because something inside her felt instinctively that this was her destiny. That night she crawled into bed knowing, in her heart and in her body that this was the man she would marry. She lay there for hours unable to talk, sleep, move; bewildered at the very thought of it all, but also sure of it in a way she had never been sure of anything else in her life.

Several days after the letter was delivered, Lynda was called away to work at the Holiday Inn, in Sarnia; a few hours north. It was a temporary position that would take her away from home for several weeks. The timing was excellent, since it would allow her some space to be alone with her thoughts and make plans for the future. In Sarnia, she wrote to her prospective husband and agreed that she would marry him. In her youthful naïveté, she had the idea he might send her flowers. Each day she expected a bouquet to appear in her room — how little she understood her future spouse in those days.

In Sarnia, she received a letter from her now-betrothed. This time Thomas expressed himself without restraint; he was thrilled, overwhelmed, overjoyed. He could scarcely believe she had agreed to be his wife. He further explained that upon returning home from the post office he had experienced such a terrible headache, he was obliged to go straight home to bed. He did not explain that he was prone to migraines at the time, so Lynda was left to interpret the headache for herself.

Her parents were devastated on hearing the news. Her father, Abe, was especially upset by this news. Though it was well-known that Thomas was a kind of religious fanatic and had a family that resembled the most monstrous of train wrecks, it was primarily his age that offended her parents. The abysmal state of affairs was then also multiplied many times by their first official meeting, which went worse than anyone might have predicted.

Thomas himself would be the first to admit to his regrettable behaviour at the dinner table of Lynda's mother and father. Her mother did her best to keep peace at the table as Thomas blathered on about the superiority of his religion, insulting their Mennonite ways. Not only did he neglect to show the minutest bit of respect to his future in-laws, but it accidently slipped out that he wished to marry Lynda within the year, since it would make him eligible for a tax break.

By then Abe was shaking with fury. "What!" he bellowed. "You want to marry my daughter to get a tax break?" His high-mindedness and superiority had pushed Lynda's father to his limit.

Here was a man nearly the same age as himself, coming into his own home, insulting his way of life and then, as if he could be insulted further, claiming his youngest daughter for his own.

Thomas only aggravated the situation by rehearsing the doctrines of the Brethren at the table, contradicting everything that was sacred about the Mennonite ways. It was not that Abe was a religious man; in fact it was his wife who kept the family's divine deliverance in careful order. By the Mennonite definition, Abe was quite a worldly man. It was known that he had brothers who smoked, a practice that caused some stir in the church. His sons could testify that he drank alcohol on the sly and, later in life they would even suspect he might not have been entirely loyal to his wife. Not only did they have a television in their home, but occasionally Lynda's brothers would also sneak into the cinema only to find their father seated in the next row.

Abe was not an intellectual man; he had little interest in religious doctrines. In his eyes, Thomas would have been a certified religious nut; exactly the sort of crazy bible thumper who knocks on doors in the middle of the afternoon and refuses to be sent away. Abe took it upon himself to consult a lawyer in hopes he might be able to prevent the marriage from going forward. However, since Lynda had reached age of majority by then there was nothing either the lawyer or Abe could do. As the situation progressed and plans for marriage continued, poor Abe became so aggrieved that he suffered a complete mental breakdown and was obliged to check himself into the hospital for several days. Though she was no more in favour of the match than her unfortunate husband, Mary did her best to hold the family together. She worried for her daughter; that she was simply being called in to rescue a family in tatters, which was true, essentially. In many ways

Lynda really was their saviour; she brought life and happiness, direction, purpose, and meaning back into the house.

It was Thomas' former mother-in-law who had made the match. She lived in the house adjacent to Thomas', and had met Lynda at their Sunday gatherings. Tom's children were also highly in favour of the match. However extreme the upheaval and disappointment in Lynda's family, it was offset by the excitement of Thomas' family, who were ecstatic at the idea of a new mother.

The upheaval on the other side was undoubtedly major. There would be no peace at her parent's home until the matter was settled and Lynda had evacuated the household. With her father in the hospital, the tension was palpable. By the time her wedding day arrived, she'd suffered such incredible stress that her slight frame had shrunk to a waif-like ninety-five pounds. No matter how troublesome and chaotic the consequences of her decision to marry Thomas, she never second-guessed herself.

From the courtship to the ceremony to the early days of their marriage, there was an unmistakable absence of romance. Mercifully, Lynda was sheltered enough that she hardly knew the difference. She was, however, wise enough to know that she wasn't in love. If she had thought about it, which she didn't, she would also have known that her betrothed was also not in love with her. Mennonite women were not trained to think in that way. What was more important was that he was an honest man who owned a home, lived by the bible and was willing to love and take care of her. Thomas Knapp, by all accounts, was *Mr. Good Enough.*

He couldn't have been in love with her, really. They still hadn't shared even one long conversation. They'd never been on a date, never stayed up until 4:00 a.m. eating crackers and drinking wine. They had never shared their fears or dared to give voice to their dreams. Mennonites are not taught to dream and neither were the Brethren. It was not their way. Never once did they broach the subject of the death of his first wife, Doris, though it must've been very fresh in his mind.

~

Thomas would not consent to being married by a minister; he had ideas about religious institutions. With both families in such an extreme state of affairs, it was deemed inappropriate to have a wedding, and so they were married at the Courthouse. The judge who married them was perceptibly drunk, a habit for which he would later be disbarred. Even Lynda was worldly wise enough to note his tattered clothing, the light coating of dandruff on his suit, and the faint smell of booze on his breath.

Even under these, the most regrettable of circumstances, her mother prepared a turkey dinner with all the trimmings, welcoming both families into her home for a reception. They did their best to enjoy the meal under the circumstances and it was not entirely a flop. Thomas's family was so obviously grateful at having a new female head of household. The dinner ended abruptly when the hospital called to inform Mary that her husband was ready to be discharged from the hospital. She shooed both families out of the house with as much love and diplomacy as she could manage, but there was no denying the sad state of affairs.

Sex was not something freely discussed among Mennonite women, married or otherwise. Nor was Thomas an especially gentle or empathetic man. They spent their wedding night across the border, since the dollar was strong and motels were less expensive there. The evening was characteristically devoid of romance; devoid even of kind words, a cup of something warm, and a modicum of tenderness. In the morning there was no breakfast or even celebratory coffee. Thomas insisted they stop at the grocery store on the way home so they might take advantage of low-priced American groceries. With her stomach as empty as her heart was overloaded, Lynda did her first shopping trip as a married women and instant mother of three. It was a fine initiation to the life she'd signed up for. Her husband was not a sympathetic man; he didn't go in for any sentimentality. But they were married now. What else was there for her to do than to be his wife?

Her husband's teenage sons were still at home in those days. His eldest daughter, Peggy, who was just three years younger than her new stepmother, had only recently left home to study nursing in Ottawa. The youngest was in and out of juvenile detention for months at a time. He'd spend a few months at home before he would eventually be caught performing another B&E at one of the local pharmacies, a stunt he pulled on several occasions. What use he had for the stolen pharmaceuticals was anyone's guess; such things were not discussed in the Knapp home.

This is not to say that Lynda had no relationship with the boys. On the contrary, she had a wonderful friendship with the youngest, in particular. Often they would stay up until the early hours of the morning, talking, telling stories, and sharing all sorts of interesting and exotic foods. They were not so very far apart in years, after all. As for the middle child, he kept very much to himself. She would often act as an intermediary between father and son. As usual, Thomas was not overly interested in the day-to-day activities of his offspring, or even the well-being of his wife, for that matter (*This has all happened before ...*). The boys concluded any family business via their stepmother.

In the Belly of Oz

Peggy visited often and became a great friend of Lynda's. The closeness in their ages made for an easy friendship and they grew to love each other dearly. Peggy was angry about Thomas's failures as a father. No one blamed him for Doris's death, but other than earning an income, he'd done little to make the home a comfortable place. He was in the habit of bellowing and preaching to anyone who would listen, and forever carrying on about the Brethren; their prejudices, their sins, and their worldly flaws. His frequent fits of disapproval caused great disturbance in the household.

It was not that he was a bad husband; Lynda eventually grew to love him, as he also grew to love her. He was a good provider and worked hard to give his family simple comforts. He never drank or swore or hit; even in the heat of his wild tirades and conniption fits, he never once laid a hand on his wife in anger. For the most part, he just wasn't paying attention. His mind was fixed on his great calling.

~

If you notice any young Mennonite girls frolicking in their home-sewn dresses on a Sunday afternoon, long-sleeved in the beating hot sun, their faces are like anyone else's; some are sad, some are smiling, some are pouting, some are laughing. They're just kids just like any other kids. Eventually they will find sturdy Mennonite spouses and who's to say they will be any less happy with their pierogies, their needlework, and their dealcoholized beer.

Like my mother, some will break free because, as we have seen, history repeats itself. Some might even find that life is not necessarily any better outside the compound. It has the same challenges, the same rewards, and the same disappointments;

the same guilty pleasures, the same cruelty, and the same beauty. And you're just as likely to wind up in a suburban home with a husband and a couple of kids you never signed up for. You're also just as likely to love them and laugh with them as you are to a quarrel and collide with them. We all make the choice, in the end.

Seventeen Years

I got a girl pregnant at nineteen. We were just kids back then. My Dad didn't believe me when I told him we were expecting twins. He said, "put Arely on the phone." I guess he needed to hear it from the source for it to be true. Except it was, and we went through with it anyway.

I was wild back then, handsome too. I never had any trouble with women. But from the day she fell pregnant, I said, "Okay, that's it, it's all over now." And I was loyal to her, body and soul, for seventeen years.

I gave my family seventeen years. For almost two decades I worked six days a week and came home every evening. Maybe in the end I was lazy. I could've helped out around the house more, could've done more yard work and less gambling. But I worked hard and I was tired. Understand I'm far from perfect.

Ninety-eight percent of the time we were happy. We maybe fought two percent of the time, and never in front of the kids. We'd go outside and talk it out on the back porch. I yelled. I got cranky sometimes. Understand I worked hard.

For six months I pulled all the overtime hours I could get. I saved $8000 and gave it to my wife, said, "Here, go to Peru, enjoy yourself." She was gone two months. Two months of no responsibilities and no one to answer to. Maybe she got a *glimpse of her life without a husband or children and she liked it. After all she missed out on her twenties.*

I hit her one time. The day my Dad died. After we got the call she just kept saying, "Don't worry, don't worry, it'll be all right." But I knew it wouldn't. I knew he was dead. She started acting up, nagging me, and so I slapped her across the face. I'm not proud of it. It's the only time I ever did that. Now she tells people I used to bash her, like I was some kind of animal.

My Dad had a heart attack on the tennis court midway through a match. We hadn't spoken for two years. But then after his attack we started talking again. We had a fight on the phone a few days before he died. He was a good man, my Dad. He worked hard. He used to tell me I was soft. He was always disappointed in me. One time he broke my nose. You can see it's crooked now. My sister too, she used to say, "You're smarter than me, Matthew." I guess she was disappointed in me too. I was always closer with my Mum.

~

People say you don't know about love until you have children. And it's true. For two years I stayed home with them. They were just little then. My wife wanted to work. So I quit my job and took care of the kids. For the first two months I hated every minute of it. I hated it. But once I settled in I loved it — best two years of my life. I used to chase them around the yard for hours, get 'em all tired out. In the evening they'd take turns lying on my back while we watched TV.

When they were little I could tell them anything. I used to read them stories. They'd just look up at me with those big eyes and listen like it was the greatest story they'd ever heard. We were so close back then. I was their Dad.

Now they're teenagers and you can barely get two words out of them. "Yeah Dad, uh-huh, Dad, okay I'm watching TV I gotta go." They wear these ridiculous shorts pulled up so high they look like Steve Erkel. Their mother won't discipline them; she's their "friend." They shit me, those two. But I love 'em. I can't help it. End of the day they're my girls; I'd do anything for them.

So I go to work every day and I put in the hours. I have to work; they'll be at Uni soon. I'll have to buy them cars so they can get to school, pay for their education. The house is nothing fancy but it's expensive. We live in a good neighbourhood. Then there are insurance and cell phones and fuel and electric bills. It never ends. I have to work.

~

In the end she took everything. She said she wouldn't fight me if I gave her the house at Callala Beach – half to her and half to the girls. So I agreed. I didn't have the energy to fight anyway. But I did fight; I fought for her. For months I left flowers at her door every single day. My girls encouraged me, they said, "Don't give up, Dad."

They lived with me, the girls. My wife wanted to party and go wild. She never got to do that. She spent her twenties raising kids.

In later years, she started going to the gym three times a day. She took steroids too, called them vitamins in front of the girls. They're not stupid; they knew. She made new friends too, started hanging out with all these body builders. I was away on business on Christmas Island when she called one night, said she was leaving me, that she was in love with her personal trainer. I got on the next flight home. She played it all casual. "It's just infatuation," she said. "He reformed my body."

She tells her parents I bashed her, that I forced drugs on her. She reckoned she had to leave for the safety of the kids; I was so moody, she was afraid for them. Understand I made mistakes. I wasn't perfect. Sometimes I did get moody. I hit her once, ten years ago. Just once. But we were happy most of the time.

Now she won't return my calls unless it's about the girls. She still has that jersey my Dad gave me; it's one of the only things he left me. But she never calls me back. She racked up $10,000 on my credit card. I paid it. I'm tired of arguing. I just want to sign the papers and be done with it.

I'll always love her though; I'm not gonna lie. She gave me my children.

~

I took the job up north for me. It was my turn to have some time for myself. For a whole year I did everything. I cooked and I cleaned, did the girl's laundry and ironed their uniforms. And I still put in twelve-hour days, six days a week.

Even up north I was so unhappy. I would leave work and drive half an hour to get cell reception, just so I could hear her voice. When I met Amy I thought it was just a moment, a blip. Just one night and that would be that. But then there I was driving home from work the next day and our wedding song came on. And instead of thinking about my wife, I thought about her. Out of nowhere, I was happy again.

I am so afraid to invest again. I couldn't let myself love her. Because I can't, I can't get hurt again. Honestly, I'd rather die. So I begged, pleaded with her not to hurt me, and when I got really scared I would push her away.

At night if I rolled over and she wasn't there, I'd get up, get dressed and go looking for her. I was working so hard, a hundred and eighty hours a fortnight, easily. Sometimes during the night it was hard to tell between sleep and awake. At 3:00 a.m. she'd get up and go to the bathroom but in my dream she'd be gone for hours and I was sure she'd been with someone else. So I'd sit up in bed and demand to know where she had been.

I hate hurting her. Her top lip starts to quiver and it just kills me. I can't stand to see her cry. I can't stand it. Making her happy, that's what's important. But understand, my wife, she really did a number on me.

I miss my family bad. I don't think about it for too long. For seventeen years I always put them first, always put their happiness before mine. She was a good mother, my wife. If I had an early start, she'd get up at 5:00 a.m. and make my toast and coffee. We were happy. She just changed, I guess.

Amy lives in a dream world. She dreams about solar eclipses and shooting stars. I just worry that I can't give her all that. I want to give her everything. I want to take care of her. I just hope she understands the reality of things. I have to work. I'm not rich.

She thinks everything will be perfect. I just worry I won't be enough for her. I'm not a musician. I didn't go to college. I like to stay at home and watch sport.

We're just going to take it slow. End of the day, you don't know what will happen. We've got five months before she has to go back. No matter what, she changed me; made me so happy. Maybe I'll go to Canada. But after the way it ended with my wife it's hard to put any stock in the future. Reality is Amy might meet someone else.

Is she really who she says she is? Does she really love me? You just don't know. I thought I knew my wife. I was loyal for seventeen years. I was always going overseas. There were brothels everywhere, you know. I never strayed. Maybe I should've been like other men.

I still hold myself back sometimes. It's hard to let go and just be...

The Year We Broke Free

The thing about divorce is that it throws a big black curtain over everything and you can't see a metre in front of your own face. In the absence of any alternative, you just stick your hands out in front of you and fumble around blindly until you find the light. When you find that light, you have to seize it with both hands, and let the idea of it serve as the catalyst for change — the rock to which you will cling as you soldier boldly back into the brightness.

When my mother left her 25-year marriage to the father of her six children, no one waited for the fire of the cannon before shooting out of the gate, hurling themselves into the darkness and deliriously flailing around for the light. Like birds suddenly and miraculously liberated from their cages, they flew madly, wildly, boldly, without direction or purpose except to fly and be free, to test their newfound wings.

~

As luck would have it, all six of those baby birds were away when Lynda finally worked up the nerve to tell her husband she was leaving him. She thanked God over and over that her children's roaming gypsy spirits kept them out of the house as Thomas paced across the living room and raged for two days straight.

She never used the word "divorce" in that fateful conversation and yet the subtext was written on the wall. Though she called it a separation, no one would have expected reconciliation, least of all Thomas. The house was sold and the furniture divided. No courts were involved; Tom and Lynda weren't the type and anyway the house was their only asset so the simplest thing to do was to split it down the middle. It sold almost immediately — something everyone involved regarded as miraculous since, a decade earlier, in the early nineties, it had been on the market for over a year and had failed to attract a single offer.

∼

With the proceeds from the sale, she put a down payment on a house in the nearby city of St. Catharines. The house on Beecher St. was fairy tale flawless, its quiet charm and historic elegance resembling a child's dollhouse; it had all the perfection of a newly whitewashed picket fence. The second floor of the house was renovated and rented out to students in order to make the mortgage payments. The rather large dining room on the main floor was fully enclosed and would serve just fine as a master bedroom.

As for her children, five out of the six of them had long since fanned out across the globe. There'd been a sort of diaspora when the eldest had turned eighteen, and the lot of them had shaken off the religious tyranny of their childhood home...

The house on Beecher St. had invisible, electromagnetic powers and with the strength of its gravitational pull, the rest of the children came home. Not to the house specifically, though one or two of us did move in temporarily. Beecher St. became the hub around which the family would now orbit. As the youngest, I took a room in the basement, where I slept on a mattress under the stairs. As a tempestuous teenager, this suited me just fine. We lived there a year before we eventually sold the house, a year we would later refer to as both the best and worst of our lives.

In the absence of our father there were no longer any rules or religious procedures to speak of at the house. Unaccustomed to so much freedom, the lot of us ran absolutely wild. With the exception of our mother and my oldest brother, we performed like a pack of wild animals darting out of their cages and crashing into things. Though Lynda did her best to keep our feet on the ground, she had other things on her mind.

~

No longer held hostage to the roles of church, kitchen, and children, she began building a life outside the dogma and judgement to which she had grown accustomed. Foremost on Lynda's mind was establishing a career. As wife to Thomas, she'd earned at most $12,000 a year. Following the purchase of the Dollhouse she had socked away the remains of her fortune, buying herself time while she buried her head in the books.

In the meantime, the eldest of her children stepped in as patriarch, a role he'd played in the past. To Lynda, he was mentor and supporter, and for his siblings, he did them the service of keeping his nose clean, both literally and figuratively, as well as providing counsel, employment, even food and shelter. More crucially, he represented strength and wisdom in a time when both were in short supply. Though such truths were hardly self-evident at the time, together Lynda and Tom Jr. would lead their pack through the woods to victory.

~

Our family was undoubtedly broken; so broken we could scarcely look after each other. Yet a current of mutual love and compassion was raging among us like a river. And as we began digging deeper into our own darkness, it was love that would hold us together.

The second of Lynda's four sons lived just down the road, where he rented a one-bedroom apartment with his wife and two young children. The apartment wasn't totally functional as a living space; to access the bedroom you had to cross a public corridor that was shared with all of the building's tenants. Not only were you forever locking and unlocking the doors, but if ever you had to use the bathroom in the middle of the night, you'd have to either throw on a robe or risk getting caught scurrying around the building half-naked in the middle of the night.

For the most part, my brother and his young family were happy and managed to keep their heads above water. He'd taken a job as a tradesman and was briefly stationed in Ecuador. Our world had cracked open so magnificently; it seemed to affect us all with tunnel vision, making it hard to see beyond our own makeshift universes. And so when this brother of mine, formerly a respectable tradesman, started up an illegal taxi service after returning from South America, no one said anything. And when the taxi service became a bootlegging service providing its after-hours clientele with cases of beer and cheap native cigarettes, no one really raised any specific objections.

His wife, however, must have had an opinion because occasionally she would leave him temporarily and without any warning. She'd pack her bags and take the kids to live at some undisclosed location. Our family isn't the sort of family to ask a lot of questions. When his wife came back we would welcome her with open arms, and she would be over at Beecher St. helping prepare Sunday dinner as though she'd never left. Then a few months later she would leave again.

~

Like any family tottering on the edge of catastrophe, there was an excess of drinking and partying and raucous karaoke nights attended by the entire clan. More menacingly though, there was substantial use of illegal drugs.

Amidst all the trials and threats of extinction, we would gather together and throw our arms in the air while we danced on our own burning ashes. Years later we would look back and it would be hard to tell which moments were celebrating newfound joy and which moments were caught in the grip of unimaginable struggle.

It would be hard to call anyone the instigator, since each of my siblings seemed to find their chosen substance of their own accord. The bootlegging business eventually spiralled into a string of business endeavours. each more corrupt than the last. This did little to aid the well-bring of either the proprietor, his siblings, or his progeny, monetarily or otherwise.

Another of my brothers had packed his opiate addiction in a suitcase and brought it back with him all the way from the west coast to our house in Ontario. He kept to himself more than any of us; played his cards close to his chest. Hardly ever could anyone say where he was at any given time or what sort of work he was doing, but there was a commonly held belief that he was living in a motel room with a woman called Suzanne, who was twice his age.

~

Much of our degeneracy was conducted in the shed, a miniature barn-like structure behind the house. My sister and I drove down to the Salvation Army, where we bought a few beat-up armchairs, a coffee table and some electric space heaters which were used to convert the shed into a bona fide den of iniquity, the likes of which our father could not have imagined in his wildest dreams.

The shed was like a sub-hub where all of us children could go and do things we did not wish for the world to witness, least of all our mother. During the day it was used as the family smoke pit but would devolve rapidly with each passing hour. I would have extended "sleepovers" that saw entire weekends passed in the shed puffing on cigarettes and crystal meth with my wayward teenage friends. With the shelter and relative comfort that the shed provided, the two of us could sit up for entire 48-hour stretches without risk of discovery.

In one particularly vexing instance, two of my siblings went back to the shed to find a third sitting alone with the lights off and the doors shut, his body trembling and his eyes bugging out of his head, trained on the mountain of cocaine spread all over the table in from of him. It was like a scene from *Scarface*. He was mumbling to himself as he rocked back and forth, though it was impossible to tell what he was going on about. They shut the door and went back up to the main house. True to form, they asked no questions.

That same sibling was soon afterwards accosted by the police while driving his car in the wrong direction down a one-way street. It couldn't possibly have escaped the officer's notice that the driver hadn't slept in days and was just a gram's throw from an overdose, his eyes once again streaked with red and bugging out for a mile. Not only had my brother left his driver's license at home but the registration on his car had been expired for some months. In the back of his Ford Festiva were at least a dozen cases of Molson Canadian and (though the cop was surely unaware) under the seat a freezer bag full of marijuana. Overwhelmed, the cop gave him a stern lecture and a ride home.

That would have been what they call hitting rock bottom, except that there was no subsequent bouncing to the surface. At the time, the star of that scene had been more of less permanently abandoned by his wife and children, who by then had been shipped off to their maternal grandparents in Saskatchewan where they were later adopted and given a new last name. In a move worthy of daytime television, his wife took up with his (now former) best friend, with whom she would eventually give birth to a third child.

~

Lynda treaded carefully and managed her brood with unqualified grace. For the most part her children were loving and respectful, however they made no attempt to disguise their skulduggery. The madness of the family was uniformly conducted out in the open. It's possible that it was the openness that ensured the survival of the family unity. While her family would never flagrantly pass their poisons amongst one another, no one ever attempted to skirt around the subject in conversation.

There were nights we'd go "dancing" until well past sunset, each taking turns sneaking off to the toilets to perform our secret mischief. Only once were we busted by our mother for such behaviour, in an episode that caused us to feel such deep shame it must have propelled at least one of us into sobriety, if only temporarily.

But Lynda was not a disciplinarian when it came to her children. It was her husband that had played the role of rule-maker and she was not about to follow his example. She'd been well versed in the stringent application of biblical morality in her children's lives and saw no benefit in applying such methodology. So rather than impose punishment she chose to simply love more and pray for a miracle.

~

Every so often my father would show up at the house on Beecher St. If he felt out of place on my mother's turf, he didn't show it. From time to time, he would even attempt to impose himself on her new way of life. The evolution of his former spouse's confidence and sense of self-possession could be directly observed by her manner of conducting such situations.

For the inaugural Christmas on Beecher St., we erected our first ever Christmas tree. None of us were well versed in such things, having been denied them for so many years, and had selected a plastic tree along with decorations from the local second hand shop. Not only was it visibly lopsided, but it was also missing a portion of its base so that it was forever tumbling over in the middle of the living room. Still the tree was loved because of what it represented. Upon discovery of the scandalous conifer, Father said flatly, "I see you have your idol," to which Lynda replied simply, "you can leave now."

Another Sunday afternoon, our father arrived at the front door. As usual, Lynda was preparing a large meal, which the family would sit down to later in the evening. When she inquired as to his activities of the day, he replied rather accusingly, "I've been doing the Lord's work." A switch flew open somewhere inside her and she replied, "That's what I'm doing too." What she understood in that moment was that this so-called Lord's work was not about the edification of all that is worldly and sinful, but rather all that is loved and worth loving.

~

The prevailing sentiment over the course of that year was emotional unrest and confusion. The burden of having to work things out on our own was sometimes onerous after having been told what to believe and how to feel for so many years. We were finding ourselves in a way we hadn't previously had the occasion to do. And though the experimentations with alternative lifestyles led several of us down many dark alleyways, starting with but not limited to substance abuse, it also in many ways brought us to a higher consciousness.

Our mother was the crusader in affairs of the spirit and showed us how to parlay our religious education into a better understanding of our inner selves and to find truth outside of the church. Most importantly she brought us all together in a time when circumstances were contriving to keep us apart. Sunday dinners became a new religious tradition and one that was not considered proper to miss. Since everyone observed this rule so vociferously, any one of us would have felt personally insulted if another absented his or herself for the table on the Sabbath.

More than a few people not directly related to our family were often in attendance at these dinners and the house became a kind of shelter for homeless birds and birds with damaged pinions. We drank wine with our meals, something we'd never have dared do when our patriarch was present, and for the first time, we shared real, uncensored conversation about worldly things, not necessarily personal things but important issues about which we felt strongly.

~

There was one Sunday dinner that I remember more vividly than any other. My eldest brother had arrived early in the afternoon, accompanied by the girl he was seeing at the time. Her name was Lily. It was sunny in the yard and Lily had brought along a bottle of cucumber wine. We ate hors d'oeuvres in the backyard and sipped on the wine, which had a faint taste of berries. There must have been nearly a dozen of us at Beecher St. that weekend, because there was traffic in and out of the side door that led from the backyard into the kitchen.

Our dog was still alive back then, though she was on her last legs. She wheezed and panted, hardly able to breathe as she lay at our feet; not for the tidbits we'd drop under the table but for the reassuring sounds and smells of our family. As usual, there was laughter at the dinner table and a feeling of comfort and togetherness; the likes of which had never been felt under our father's jurisdiction. There was no pounding of the heart if someone wanted to play loud music or use foul language. Once and for all, we were free.

~

The sale of the Dollhouse on Beecher St. was finalised a month before the last of the liquid cash ran out. My mother and I moved to a quiet townhouse on the edge of the city, which she was renting at the time, but would purchase in the years to come. The rest of my siblings were cut loose. It was an expedient conclusion to the mad flight for freedom, and the time had come for the six of us to forge our own paths, find new branches to rest upon.

That we survived the year on Beecher St. is no small miracle. That no one landed in hospital or in prison, even more so. Some people might call it luck but we are not those sorts of people. Looking back on that time in our lives, it is clear that *someone* or *something* was looking out for us, that we were protected by divine forces in ways we are only now just beginning to understand.

~

People offer expressions of pity when you tell them your parents are divorced. They'll say, "gosh, that's sad" or "wow, that must have been hard." Matthew gets this all the time and in his case, maybe it is a real tragedy. His family was a happy one most of the time.

But my parent's divorce wasn't sad. It gave both parties a chance to start over again, to build a life that was free from the boundaries of each other. My father was relieved from the financial pressure of supporting a family and with the sale of our house, he was finally able to retire — at seventy years old he too found freedom. My mother, who was not yet fifty, got a chance to not only explore but thrive in the big open world her husband had long denied her.

What you can't see in the thick of it all are the incredible possibilities such a situation provides. You look around and you see all these newly formed holes in your life and so you fill those spaces with your despair. But what you don't feel under the weight of that despair is your enormous capacity for change. Even if change is the last thing on your mind when you're on the receiving end of a separation, the adaptation is a necessary enterprise from which you will inevitably emerge stronger, more malleable, and able to live with more humanity.

That's the thing about families; they grow and change and mold into whatever cast you forge for them. There are no shortcuts or bridges over the emotional stumbling blocks along the way, you just have to put your head down and barrel ahead the best you can. Every mile will be shorter than the last and eventually there will start to be light in your tunnel. Years later you'll look back and see it for what it was; a necessary stopover on the way to your true station — the one you're at home in today — the blessed present moment.

The Meaning of Family

Much like family, football means something different depending who you ask. To Americans, it's gridiron: bulky strongmen running around in metres of Styrofoam and spandex pants. To Europeans, it's soccer, also recognised as football by urban Canadians trying to sound cultured. To Australians, it's rugby league, rugby union, and also AFL (and sometimes GayFL, depending on what state you're from). To me, a Canadian who was raised on Robert Schumann and Laura Ingalls Wilder, it's tight bodies, burly Islanders, and sweat — a lot of it.

Jean-Marc used to say that the objectification of the opposite sex was an activity reserved exclusively for men. He believed that women, while appreciating the male form, selected their partners based on criteria that were more subjective. He may have been on to something with that bit about selecting partners, but as far as objectively admiring the male form, I respectfully disagree. Women do this all the time, which leads me to the following guilty confession: I love rugby.

It's only fair that the women of Australia should be offered compensation for the loss of spousal companionship four nights a week, eight months a year. What else could explain shirts *that* tight and shorts *that* short? Almost nothing is left to the imagination. The striped jersey hugs the footballer's figure in such a way that you can almost feel the tautness of slippery skin and pulsating arteries beneath a thin blanket of synthetic fabric. And the shorts...ah! The shorts should have their own television show.

Occasionally Matt and I go to games on weekends. Two months into the season, I have a rudimentary understanding of the game; enough at least to know that the idea is to score a "try," which is not the same as a "goal," that the penalty box is called the "sin bin" and it's actually just the locker room. Matthew is beside himself in frustration that I persist in making homoerotic jokes and tapping him on the shoulder asking him to explain aspects of the game that, in his mind, he has already explained over and over. The trouble is that I don't speak rugby. Matthew's explanations are in a language I don't understand so we just keep going back and forth like this:

"Why are they letting him run like that? What don't they tackle?"

"I *told* you this, sweetheart. You're not *listening*. The Saints kicked the ball past the try line so the Doggies get a free tap on the twenty."

"Right, thanks." That makes sense then. A free tap on the twenty. Okay, I think, more confused than ever.

Of course, Matt will get his revenge once the game really gets going. The ugly secret he's been keeping from me for five months now is that, at football games, he's *that* guy — the one who jeers at the opposing team, calls them names, and mocks their bad habits. He yells instructions at the top of his lungs until his voice gets scratchy and dry. Subtly as possible, I sink further into my chair and lean away, attempting to save my eardrums any further damage. His wild shouting has turned my hearing all fuzzy, like a speaker system turned up too loud. Thankfully he's not the *only* guy. Many Australians do this, even middle-aged ladies with packs of young children. At least five in our immediate vicinity are eating meat pies, drinking bourbon, and yelling like the place is on fire.

~

Like football, family is a different game for everyone involved. Sometimes your own teammates are playing by an entirely different set of rules. And like that very same game, my family has seen a thousand different variations, prospering and failing in proportion to the size and restrictions of the playing field. Family is elastic; it moves and shapes according to our needs and desires. Ours is non-partisan; we are emancipated, lionhearted, wild.

Matt's family is not as stretchy. It kept its shape so long and stretched itself so fast that its seams came clean apart. For him, there is only one kind of family: the kind that gets married and stays married no matter what. There aren't a lot of divorcées in his immediate circle; divorce is still talked of as though it were a great tragedy. When a man they know leaves his wife for a woman he met in Thailand who's half his age, they are beside themselves with pity for the poor, hapless woman abandoned. No one wonders whether his wife might not have been glad to see him gone.

They are not in the habit of thinking this way. For Matthew, family is your wife and children in the same way that football is rugby league. Period. It's the only *real* way. The rest are only variations on the superlative, correct, most acceptable way of doing things. Family is family and anything else is compromise; the thing you settle for if Plan A doesn't work out the way you hoped it would.

It's the transitional time for his family now, which is made exponentially more difficult since they don't know what they're transitioning *to* and still longing for the thing they're transitioning out of, still looking at all the things they don't have any more rather than the things they stand to gain. There aren't any phoenixes in this family yet, no mould in which to cram the bits and pieces of their former selves, giving form and definition to their future selves. The family is left licking its own wounds, causing themselves further damage.

It's divorce. It's been ugly. Knives have been thrown — sharp ones. It was hard, messy, unexpected. It left them spiritually pale and malnourished; too much McDonald's and not enough homemade tuna casserole. Matthew worries about his girls. Constantly. *"They use their phones too much. They don't study enough. They only care about famous boy bands. They never clean their rooms. They fight all the time. This one never washed the dishes and that one called her sister a bitch. They used to be more loving. I used to be closer with them."*

Their behaviour has changed since their parents parted ways and Matthew assumes this must be the cause of it. Never mind that they are sixteen and full of hormones. It's easier for him to take the blame. Sticking it into a nice, tidy box where everything makes sense, makes it easier to understand and thus to avoid future pain. *"My daughter is rude to me because my wife was rude to me. My wife was rude to me because I did X, Y, and Z. If I avoid doing X, Y, and Z in the future, I will not get hurt this way again, my wife will not leave me and my daughter will treat me kindly."* It's simple Socratic logic that solves the entire divorce problem.

∼

The subject of my departure keeps coming up. It gets closer and closer until we can't put off talking about it any longer. I am and am not allowed to discuss my future life. For example, I might say I've decided not to sublet my apartment in September, since I will need a place to live, but I am not allowed to say that I will put my things in storage and transfer my lease before I come back to Australia. *"When I come back ..."* is not a phrase we allow ourselves to play off. It makes Matthew nervous. In another life, he planned for a future and then that future fell apart. He's more cautious now, doesn't want to set himself up for disappointment. He's seen enough of that.

He is working hard. He wakes at 4:00 a.m., sometimes six days a week, and returns home at 6:00 p.m. At home he eats dinner, watches an hour or two of television, and goes straight to bed. You can see full-body exhaustion in his posture and his halfway shut eyelids. Some days his face is so pale and his eyes so translucent you can almost see right through them. He reminds us often how hard he must work, how little time he has for fun and games, how costly it is to run the household. He's a soldier; he's got to keep fighting.

He's carrying a life that was built up by two able-bodied people; two incomes, two parents, two people to do the housework, pick the kids up from school, pay the bills, make dentist appointments and parent-teacher interviews, take the garbage out, and mow the lawn. He never sees friends anymore. There's no time for them. The only time he gets to himself are the twenty minutes between waking up and leaving for work. Everyone else in the house is sleeping at 4:00 a.m. By the time he gets home, the television is blaring, there are pots and pans banging around in the kitchen, his daughter is chatting loudly in front of her computer, and someone is almost always asking him for money.

He wants me to leave. Not to break up, but for me to leave. He thinks this will allow him to see clearer, to know if this is or is not the right thing, to see how it affects the precarious balance of his living situation. I don't know how my leaving is meant to improve things. There will be less laundry, cooking and cleaning to do, but no one around to do it. The only logic I see is that it will be one less person around for Matthew to worry about. So I'm leaving, I suppose. Anyhow, there's no other way.

Despite my reservations, that's what he's asked me to do and he hardly ever asks for anything. He's spent his life serving others. He apologizes for taking a nap, for going to bed early, for having an appointment at the bank, for taking a shower when dinner is almost ready and also for not showering before sitting down to dinner, for not taking me out on the town, for wanting McDonald's instead of more brown rice, for not finding time to change light bulbs, for not having a better car or a bigger house. If I dare to point out that he has offended me in some way, he is mortally wounded — crushed. He feels he has failed. He crawls inside himself and doesn't come out for days.

Having the house to himself for a while is meant to take some of the pressure off. So I'm going home, whatever that word means. I have so many homes now that the idea of "going home" is geographical catch-22. Which home? Montreal? St. Catharines? Canada? How can I go home when I am already home in Australia? As far as complaints go it's all very bourgeois, like complaining about having too much money. I am wealthy in homes, rich in family; I have a luxurious cushion of familial love I can "go home to" at any time. We should all be so lucky. When I get used the idea, it's not so bad.

Montreal is the shape of me. I was formed by the shores of the St-Laurence River, carved into being by the ice and snow, given definition in great halls of learning and found expressions in its libraries, coffee houses, and repertory cinemas. There's the snow, for another thing; that'll be nice. Then there is the company of friends, evenings alone at the movies, public transit, winter boots, and cocktail hour. I have a good life there.

I must be elastic too because part of me is now shaped by Australia, finding definition in a house, a person, and another way of living. But no matter how well-defined its turns and junctions, it's clear that it is not my shape. This shape is only partially mine. Some of my corners are real and some have been dented into place by a country that does not belong to me. This is not a life that I chose; it's a life that chose me.

~

It's pure coincidence that the day I meet Matthew's ex-wife is also the day he is to meet the solicitor and sign the divorce papers. I'm sitting in a café with a sheath of papers, buzzing from my second or third latté. She arrives with her daughter, who waves hello, though she herself says nothing since she doesn't recognise me, doesn't have a clue that this is the woman who is living the life she cast off, who cooks for her children, hand washes their school uniforms, and makes love to her estranged husband.

But I do, and I'm shaking like a leaf with this fact in hand. Rather than standing up and saying hello like a grown-up, I pick up a highlighter and bury my head in my papers, assuming the pose of someone who is working. But I'm not working, of course, because my brain is on fire. When she puts two and two together from the table where she is seated with her daughter, she immediately comes over and introduces herself like a proper adult, which apparently I am not, because I'm still pretending so faithfully to be concentrating on my work, my nose practically touching the table in mock fixation.

What strikes me most about her is that she is dressed exactly like me; baggy linen pants, tight sweater, brown hair tied back, friendly (if a bit exaggerated) smile. Were it not for her South American complexion, she'd look more like my sister than my own flesh-and-blood sister. And that's only the beginning of it. Every so often Matthew spirals into a panic when I have said something in the exact way his wife once did, the same expression, the same choice of words, the same delivery. I see panic in his eyes. She practices yoga and meditation. She has suffered from a similar case of extreme body fixation, sent her body to its limits with weights and training. She is health conscious to excess. She used to put vision boards up all over the house, which I almost did myself before Matt caught me in the act and the sheer horror in his face led me to reconsider. To boot, there are our names: Amy and Arely. So close it's uncanny.

She is as embarrassed as I am, apologizing profusely for not coming over earlier, politely overlooking the fact that I have been sitting here all along and I have nothing like her excuse. We apologize to one another with such profuseness and vigour that nothing really gets said, except that we should sit down and talk sometime, that the girls love me and she is happy that Matthew is happy. Her nervousness, her friendliness and her glowing face are catching; I feel all warm and comfortable, overly generous with my eyelashes — I want, no, I *need* her to like me.

Communication since the separation has been dreadful. Immediately, the former spouses launched into the verbal equivalent of a type of jungle warfare that no treaty of peace has since been able to quell. I've seen several explosive communiqués that I wish I had not. Both parties have behaved appallingly, as only a pair of future-divorcés can do.

The summer my first love broke my heart I spent composing several-thousand-word tirades condemning him as a worthless imitation of a man, sometimes more than once a week. I told him he was not worthy of love. I vowed that he would suffer more brutally than he could possibly imagine. I called him names. I told him he was a pathetic lover and that he would most certainly die alone. I didn't even have a computer; I made special trips to university libraries and public cafes to write these pitiful dispatches. In my letters, I became the worst possible version of myself.

Nice people do bad things. Who among us has not said terrible, damaging, and despicable things to someone they once loved? Being hurt by someone we love often makes us feel we have license to act like an asshole. When you get punched your instinct it to punch back — except harder and more deliberately. You want it to hurt at least as bad. It doesn't make you an asshole in life; it makes you human. When you've been around the merry-go-round a few times, you learn how to get your heart broken with dignity. The first time is always the ugliest, the most bloody, and leaves you with the deepest scars. Being in your thirties doesn't seem to make it any easier. It may even be worse, since you're more clever in the ways you damage your partner, knowing their weak spots as well as you know your own.

It's important to acknowledge that what is true for one person is not necessarily true for both parties. *Reality*, if there ever was such a thing, is what you believe most firmly in your heart to be true. Wife declares husband an asshole; husband maintains he was not an asshole. Both are correct. Wife declares husband an abusive, deadbeat gambler; husband counters with profusions of loyalty, hard work, and dedication. Both are a subjective interpretation of facts and both are correct. What is real for one is for the other no more than her imagination. Imagination, after all, is also reality, especially in dealing with the past.

Matthew is deeply disturbed by the idea of Arely and me sitting down to anything at all, be it a coffee, a quick chat, or a metaphorical game of cards. He has her all figured out. He is convinced she is trying to win my loyalty, to show me the truth in her version of things. He is beside himself with anxiety. Sick with anxiety. For the ensuing week, life is a game of painful speculation. At night he dreams of piranhas eating the faces off the people he loves. He dreams he is at a theme park punching up one of the carnies until his nose is broken and bloody. Suddenly he is so much more tired. Evenings I find him cross-legged on the bedroom floor. Head in hands, he says, "I'm tired of chasing my tail."

As if his burden was not heavy enough, today is the day he is to sign the final papers. He comes home from work early, white as a sheet, eerily quiet, not even bothering to justify his silence. There are too many reasons to feel bad today; what's the use in rhyming them off? His face is uncharacteristically empty. He feels nothing; nothing but overwhelmed, tired and overworked. He shuts himself off, slinking into an emotional hole so deep he is liable to get lost and never come out.

I walk him to the solicitor's office, at which point he starts talking again about how important it is that I go back to Canada. When prompted he cannot think of a reason why he has chosen this moment to bring the subject up again, cannot connect the dots. All he knows is that all this — this moment, this feeling, this task — hurts. He doesn't want to do *this* again. It's too painful. Ergo, he would like me to leave. He would like to be alone for a while, to process, to clear out the clutter in his mind and decide if "all this" is really worth it.

The big secret I've been keeping from the man I love the most is the thing you're never supposed to say to a person who has given his life providing others with the comforts of life: I don't care about any of it. I lived without iPhones, cable television, and good suburban neighbourhoods for a long time and I could do it again. Back home my apartment has mice and costs me five hundred a month. I chop vegetables and prepare food on a slab of recycled wood that sits on top of a washing machine that only works half of the time. I bought most of the artwork at garage sales for five bucks a piece. It's ugly and it suits the place. My friends call it "Peewee's Playhouse." Most of my furniture comes from a sweet little store called the side of the road.

I'm no Mother Theresa; I need a roof over my head, central heating, and a flushable toilet. Sometimes I dream of better things: bigger homes, nicer paintings on the walls, and tiles without cracks. I'm not above it all, but I'm not willing to sacrifice *living* for *owning*. There has to be more to life than three-bedroom townhouses.

Now I have seen what it takes for a grown man to carry a family and give them everything the world tells him he is obliged to give them, I want no part of it. Where is it written that the definition of family includes a house and three cars and a husband who works eighty hours a week? Where is it written that the children must have access to four hundred channels, the latest iPhone, and fifty dollars a week?

What good is the stuff when it comes at such a high price? What about freedom? How is a person to enjoy her freedom at the expense of her lover's? Matthew works and work and works so that in a few years he will be able to buy a house, for which he will be obliged to work and work some more. Eventually he will get old enough to retire, at which point he will allow himself to relax, although after denying himself a life for so many years, who can say whether or not he will remember how one actually goes about "living." It's all very harrowing to think about.

~

Our life together unravels slowly at first, but the twisting and turning begin to gain momentum until eventually we are careening out of control, a ball of string tumbling down a staircase, growing smaller at every turn, tumbling further and further until we are nothing but two lonely piles of string, looking up from the bottom of a deep, dark place.

There are still days when Matthew comes home smiling, but the distance between those days opens up like a great crack in the earth, separating us with our own invisible fault line. We can't get across. Where once there was laughter and heavy hearts were the exception to the rule, the opposite is now true. When he tires of this game of endurance, the suffering begins to hold. It wants to be given voice. It wants recognition. Pretty soon it takes hold of him completely, covering over all the best parts of his nature.

I'm leaving in less than two months. By now, lovemaking has gone the way of the laughter. Not even booze and expensive lingerie can call it back. There's too much in the way. Matthew's suffering is working overtime. *Recognise me! I'm working hard. Go easy on me.* A "promotion" at work turns out to be less hours and less money for a job that he hates — a bag lady in a princess gown. He's got nothing left. In the evenings, he no longer lies in bed watching me undress while we exchange the news or engage in witty repartee. He covers himself in blankets and rolls the other way, pretending not to see me.

Meanwhile, the weather grows cold. It's winter now. What of all our grand plans? Beethoven's Ninth at the Opera House, horseraces in July, Melbourne in August. Sydney isn't manifesting the way I had planned: there's never the time for dinners in the city, never the money for horse-riding in national parks, never the energy for picnics on the beach. All that gets tucked away into a drawer of forgetting. I haven't met any of Matthew's friends or made any of my own. Sightseeing alone depresses me. The Museum of Contemporary Art isn't nearly as much fun when you don't have someone with whom to poke fun at the crazy light installations and ugly sculptures.

The more nights we spend eating Chinese take-out and watching MTV, the clearer it becomes that this is not my life. This is Matt's life. I squeezed myself into it but it doesn't fit me properly. It's a dress that I can pull over my head and stick my arms through but it looks all funny and lumpy. It doesn't flatter me at all. I squawk and stamp my feet like a frustrated child. I'm supposed to be on top of the world. This isn't how the story was supposed to go.

Meanwhile, Matthew sinks deeper still. His gambling grows more frequent, until he's at the betting shop almost every day. What once was a bit of fun on a Saturday becomes a full-blown habit. He disappears for hours at a time, not telling me where he's going. When he runs out of money, he asks me for some of mine and becomes enraged when I refuse, as if I don't know where the money is going. He asks me to leave. Not just at the end of August when my visa expires, he wants me to leave now, a month early. He picks me up from the train station one evening, pulls the car onto the curb, and asks me plainly if I don't have somewhere else to go. This makes me furious.

The Sydney experiment has gone awry. Sometimes I am able to muster up compassion and other times I am angry and vindictive. I want him to feel very bad about this. I'm broke. I have no connections, Matthew knows that. I'm alone on the other side of the world. Where would I go? Surely I cannot go home now with my tail between my legs. I was supposed to get off that plane a brand new woman, heart a little stronger and hair a little longer. People would comment on how much I had grown and what I had achieved. This isn't the ending I had planned.

For all the drama of these brief descents into madness, even the worst eventually blows over. It doesn't take long. Except instead of coming out stronger, as the story is supposed to go, Matthew and I come out dazed and confused, tripping over each other's inflamed hearts. Perhaps it's time to go back where I came from.

The End

(and the beginning, of course, but also the end)

I wanted the ending to be beautiful. I wanted it to sing with romance. I painted a picture of it, wrote it down, planned out a sequence of events two months before it came.

My portrait was sad but full of hope. I'd bake mountains of casseroles and put them in the freezer so that Matt and the girls would have something to eat after I left, so they wouldn't eat too much McDonalds. What a good little wife I was going to be.

Next I'd strategically leave things around the house, important things, so he'd know I was planning to return. I'd hide some books or a sweater in the back of some shelf. I'd leave my favourite underwear in the wrong drawer, and store a box or two of clothing in the garage.

Then I'd plant notes all over the house, messages of love and encouragement, maybe even poetry. Every so often Matt would find one and be flooded with love and affection. He'd be so moved he would have to sit down at the kitchen table and catch his breath.

Lastly I would scrub the house from top to bottom, even the appliances. I was going to toss out expired things, wash and iron the linens, change light bulbs and dust overhead fans. A tidy house would be part of my legacy.

Eventually the day would come when Matt would drive me to the airport. The late August air would be damp and cold. We'd hold hands on the way but not say much, feeling instead of talking, which is how I always prefer it. At baggage check we'd laugh and hold each other while we waited in line, enjoying these last few moments. He'd walk me to security, where we'd hold each other some more, cry a little and then say goodbye.

The ending was nothing like that.

I didn't bake a single casserole, write any notes, clean any appliances, or wash any damn linens. I was done and I wanted to go home. I wanted to be where my people were. I wanted to be among friends. I wanted to start acting my age, to go out and do things, to listen to experimental string bands again and to eat poutine at 4:00 a.m.

It wasn't just the things I wanted to get to; it was also the things I wanted to get away from. I wanted to escape television. I wanted out of suburbia. I was tired of fast food and rugby. I was tired of trips to the supermarket being the highlight of my day.

~

Matthew took a month off, half of which he would spend with me and the other half alone after I left. Both of us were hoping for a renaissance. Winter in the suburbs had taken its toll. We were frustrated, each for our own reasons. The current of love that had once flowed so freely between us was languishing, drying up.

We booked a trip to Melbourne the week before I left. I was excited. Melbourne was said to be cosmopolitan and happening, like Montreal – the ideal place for Matt and I to fall back in love.

Matt spent the first night of our trip on the couch, sulking. He'd left the inaugural restaurant choice to me and I'd chosen a well-reviewed, swanky Moroccan joint I read about online. Matt hated it.

He was underdressed, to begin with, which made him uncomfortable. We dined early with the business crowd, who were still in their suits and ties, making Matt feel like a pauper in his t-shirt and jeans. He was convinced our waitress was laughing at him. He retaliated by insulting the food, the servers, and the other patrons.

He didn't recognise any of the dishes, which were unlike anything he'd ever eaten before. Australians are notoriously unadventurous when it comes to food. He kept saying that afterward we'd stop for a burger, get some *real* food. He complained that it was too expensive, that the portions were not big enough, that there was not enough meat. Every so often, he would guess how much the meal was going to cost. Five hundred? Six hundred?

It was deeply uncomfortable for both of us. Yet he kept reminding me who was picking up the bill, reminding me to be grateful. The meal was interminable. I'd chosen the table d'hôte and the dishes just kept coming. We squirmed in our chairs for what seemed like hours. At some point, I excused myself, went to the bathroom and cried. There was nothing renaissance about it.

The Moroccan fiasco came to a painful and pitiful climax as we made a game plan for the following day. Because I'd chosen the restaurant and Matt was picking up the bill, tomorrow was going to be his day. I'd had my fun and now it was his turn.

He wanted to go to the horseraces and he wanted to stay there all day. He said we should leave at noon. Five hours seemed to me like a long day at the races. I whined about this, suggesting we leave at one o'clock instead.

This made Matthew furious. The way he saw it, I was selfish and ungrateful. Wanting to leave an hour later was proof that I had no concern for the things that he wanted to do, no respect for his wishes despite how hard he had been working to support me these last six months. Here he was treating me to an expensive meal, enduring the unpleasantness for my sole benefit, and this is how I repay him? He was livid.

After that he shut down completely. He paid for our two hundred and seventy dollar meal and we walked back to the hotel in silence. This was Matthew's famous double whammy: the guilt trip followed by the silent treatment. By now this was familiar territory but it was no less effective. I felt terrible — guilty, angry, and manipulated. Matt slept on the couch and refused to talk to me, neglecting to respond to my desperate pleas and apologies.

He left the hotel early the next morning, not telling me where he was going. I ate breakfast alone and waited for him to call, which he did eventually. He'd been at the TAB, the betting shop. Gambling was Matt's answer to everything: sadness, confusion, boredom, even happiness. It was a habit he'd picked up from his father.

We met back at the hotel and talked it through. Eventually he forgave me. He had to. We had two more days in Melbourne and we had to salvage what we could. We went to the races, we shopped for the girls, and we ate at safe Italian restaurants or ordered in from the hotel bar. On the last day we split up. I visited the markets and wandered old neighbourhoods on foot while Matt went back to the TAB. In the evening we met at the casino where we ordered drinks, played cards, and played it safe. We went home sore and confused.

We did have a renaissance — sort of. The looming separation made us feel more in love, perhaps because we both feared change. The present was tolerable and safe, the future unknown. For a week we slept like it was the last night on earth, every night, huddled into each other with long faces. We had sex in a timid, slow kind of way, but there was nothing fresh or sensational about it. It was always quiet and always at night.

Toward the end Matthew changed his mind about me leaving. Suddenly he didn't need the time alone, didn't need to see what it would be like. He just wanted me to stay. Maybe it was because he knew it wasn't possible, knew I had to go home, that there was no legal way I could stay. Maybe a lot of things.

∼

The airport scene played out almost exactly the way I'd planned it. We said reassuring things to each other, made reassuring plans for the future, and cried a puddle of tears before I got on the plane.

Going back to Canada was supposed to be the end of the story. Or rather, it was supposed to be the beginning of part two. That's the way I'd planned it, anyway. Despite everything, Matt and I intended to stay together. We made loose plans for him to visit me in Canada or for me to return to Australia. I still saw Matt as my future, the place I would eventually go back to. Even if it made no sense logistically, we still had hope.

But being back home changed everything, again. The first time we spoke on the phone, after a twenty-four-hour commute across the ocean, he was sullen and quiet. He first words to me where thick with indignation, *"did you go back to Canada because of César?"*

I was floored. The suggestion was so off base, so deluded that I didn't know how to respond. This would become a pattern with us in the months that followed. Matthew was insecure and unable to trust me. It was too hard for him to be so far away. His jealousy grew and grew. As the weeks passed he continued to make wild accusations about obscure ex-lovers whose names it was amazing he could even remember.

Seeing me flourish without him was hard. He'd become attached to his role as the provider and longed to regain the comfort of mutual dependency. Meanwhile I was relishing my recovered independence. I was living again: reconnecting with friends, making sweeping life changes, moving to a new city, nurturing a social life and a new career.

I had to cut him loose. His accusations had grown more and more outlandish, losing their grounding in reality. We were dragging each other down, hanging on to a love that didn't exist anymore. Australia stopped making sense. I stopped wanting to go back.

~

With time the puzzle pieces are coming together. What I know now is how little I knew about love back then. Did we love each other or did we love what the other represented? It's hard to tell sometimes. Attachment gets to look a lot like love.

Matthew gave me the validation I badly needed at the time, made me feel like I was worth loving — at any size, in any job, without any law degrees. He gave me the fierce commitment that had previously been denied me. A future with Matt was a future that made sense to me. It made life seem certain, less scary.

Meanwhile, I represented all the things Matt had missed out on while he was raising children. Being with me made him feel young again, like he might get a second chance at being young too. It also reconfirmed his role as the provider, an important part of his identity that had been called into question by his divorce.

Being together meant we didn't have to ask ourselves any of those hard questions. It meant we could conveniently skip over that annoying business of self-love. We had each other. What else could there be? But it also meant we had to forgo the possibility of growth and change. We were too dependent on each other, too attached to allow anything like that.

It could never have worked. Not for me, anyway. I had soul work to do, and soul work can't be done without complete freedom to shapeshift at any turn. I thought that Australia was my big year of change. It wasn't. It was my big year of letting go, so I could allow myself to change. It was a crucial yet intermediary step.

Another bird went down with the same stone. That bird was the American dream. I saw what it cost and the price was too high. It was essential to cross that off my list, in order to allow for a more authentic dream. The American dream is someone else's dream.

I needed to get the idea of being "safe" out of my system. Deep down, I was still a law student, looking for a secure place in an unpredictable world. Letting go of that idea was something I had to do on my own, without anyone to hold my hand. Living is scary and dangerous, but someone's got to do it.

There are no endings, only the beginning of the next great adventure. The moments you plan for, the people you wait for and the loves you long for – they're just seeds. You can plant them and water them and pray for sun, but you never know how your garden will grow. There are too many external factors: a late frost, an onslaught of heavy rains, a plague of locusts maybe.

We have to go forward without fear, or else look our fear in the face and run toward it. We have to travel in the direction of our hearts, swim with the tide of our desires. Only there does freedom lie. Only there can we find joy.

Acknowledgements

To my beautiful sister Zion, thank you for answering my text at 4:00 a.m. and giving me the green light on an adventure that would change both of our lives. I'm honoured that you chose me for a sister.

To Matthew, for creating an adventure on top of an adventure, inviting me into your family and teaching me about rugby and racehorses. There will always be a place for you in my heart.

To Elisabeth Formosa and Laura-Alexandre Vrabie, for loving my writing through the best and worst of times. The book and I really needed that.

To Iguana Books, for asking me to change the title and cover, a bold but much-needed suggestion.

To Jay, for reading all about my sordid past and loving me anyway and not letting me throw away the paper draft.

To Pashana, for bringing me into a family that supports running wild. I honour your wisdom.

To everyone who donated to the IndieGoGo campaign, it's because of you that this book is properly edited and has an ending that doesn't stink like rotten meat.

Lastly, to life for knocking my freakin' socks off every single day. I love you so much.

Iguana Books
iguanabooks.com

If you enjoyed *In the Belly of Oz*...
Look for other books coming soon from Iguana Books! Subscribe to our blog for updates as they happen.

iguanabooks.com/blog/

If you're a writer ...
Iguana Books is always looking for great new writers, in every genre. We produce primarily ebooks but, as you can see, we do the occasional print book as well. Visit us at iguanabooks.com to see what Iguana Books has to offer both emerging and established authors.

iguanabooks.com/publishing-with-iguana/

If you're looking for another good book ...
All Iguana Books books are available on our website. We pride ourselves on making sure that every Iguana book is a great read.

iguanabooks.com/bookstore/

Visit our bookstore today and support your favourite author.

Lightning Source UK Ltd.
Milton Keynes UK
UKHW011442090720
366275UK00003B/893